THE *Sex* FILES

About the Author

Rowan Davis was born and raised on the West Coast. Hurricane Katrina, a giant leap of boredom, and a sudden rash decision took her east, where she met her husband and stepdaughter. (A Libra with a Scorpio Descendant did what?) She now lives in the state of Texas, surrounded by horses and cowboy hats.

Davis has studied metaphysical subjects for many years, concentrating on astrology and its connections to psychology. She understands that one of the chief concerns of human life is to study and know oneself, and believes that there are many ways for a person to do this. To know yourself and to help others to know and love themselves is the highest achievement a person can attain.

To Write to the Author

If you wish to contact the author or would like more information about this book, please write to the author in care of Llewellyn Worldwide and we will forward your request. Both the author and publisher appreciate hearing from you and learning of your enjoyment of this book and how it has helped you. Llewellyn Worldwide cannot guarantee that every letter written to the author can be answered, but all will be forwarded. Please write to:

Rowan Davis
℅ Llewellyn Worldwide
2143 Wooddale Drive, Dept. 987-0-7387-1354-0
Woodbury, Minnesota 55125-2989, U.S.A.

Please enclose a self-addressed stamped envelope for reply,
or $1.00 to cover costs. If outside U.S.A., enclose
international postal reply coupon.

Many of Llewellyn's authors have websites with additional information
and resources. For more information, please visit our website at
http://www.llewellyn.com.

ROWAN DAVIS

THE *Sex* FILES

Your *Zodiac* Guide to
Love & Lust

Llewellyn Publications
Woodbury, Minnesota

First Edition
First Printing, 2009

Book design and format by Donna Burch
Cover art © Kun-Sung Chung, www.kschung.com
Cover design by Ellen Dahl
Llewellyn is a registered trademark of Llewellyn Worldwide, Ltd.

Library of Congress Cataloging-in-Publication Data
Davis, Rowan.
  The sex files : your zodiac guide to love & lust / Rowan Davis. — 1st ed.
     p.   cm.
  ISBN 978-0-7387-1354-0
  1. Astrology and sex. I. Title.
  BF1729.S4D38 2009
  133.5'864677—dc22

                                                                    2008042759

Llewellyn Publications
A Division of Llewellyn Worldwide, Ltd.
2143 Woodale Drive, Dept. 987-0-7387-1354-0
Woodbury, Minnesota 55125-2989, U.S.A.
www.llewellyn.com

Printed in the United States of America

JAN ⹀ 2009

Other Books by Rowan Davis

The Ex Files

The Ex-Boyfriend Book

Contents

Aries

What You Need to Know About
an *Aries* Man

March 21–April 20

Flames on red candles shift in the breeze, wax drips like blood. He pushes you onto the bed, tears at your lips with his teeth, cradles your body in his strong arms. His desire is undeniable, and your heart pounds with a sacred beat. You are on the altar, about to be both sacrificial victim to his need and sorceress to his fantasies. He wants you. He rips the clothes from your body and from his. Your nails leave tracks down his back and he groans. He's been waiting to have you for so long, as you've been waiting for him. You are submissive in his arms, and yet somehow in control. He worships you, and you let him know with every fiber of your being how very much a man he is and how conquered you are—for the moment.

God of War Incarnate

Yep. He's the god of war, the most viral man a damsel in distress has likely come across in her entire stressful career of getting herself into trouble. You want a guy with a blazing sword? He's got one. How about a military mind full of strategy and sexy trouble-making? Uh-huh. He's just about as masculine as a human body can hope to get. Up to a point. Some Aries males rely on their physique to seduce their lovers, and some use their considerable brainpower to project their maleness at any female in sight. He's definitely a chick magnet, just like his ruling Greek god, Ares, was. (Wasn't he?) One look at the mortal god before you, and you must be convinced that his namesake Ares *had* to have gotten along with the ladies. I mean, look how that man *struts*.

Ares definitely enjoyed the job of starting wars and moving mortals about like pieces on a chessboard, but he didn't get along with the ladies. Oh, he had his affairs, but he wasn't what one would call *successful* with women—at least not in the sense that Apollo and Zeus were successful. The one love of his life was Aphrodite, a powerful, married goddess who used her physical beauty to manipulate everyone around her. It was in his love affair with

Aphrodite that the conflicts in Ares's personality became evident. He longed for dominance, but true domination comes from subjugating another dominant person—not a submissive one. He wanted a moral union, but to achieve his ideal would have meant leaving the very person he wanted it with. Most of all, he wanted the one person he could never fully have.

These conflicts are in the back of every Aries' mind, as is the fear of being caught in a humiliating act. This too is echoed in the myths of Ares. His love affair with Aphrodite became quite public when Aphrodite's husband decided to set a trap for Ares and Aphrodite. As soon as the two illicit lovers began to make love, unbreakable chains surrounded them and trapped them in the act. Aphrodite's cuckold husband then invited all of the gods to come for a look, and in the end it was Ares who was the ass for his relationship was shown in its true light—purely sexual without any of the love or commitment he hoped for.

His Top Traits Explored

He's Confident

Sure he is. On the outside, anyway. On the inside, he vacillates between being a man's man and being a cowering mass of vulnerable ego as he nervously awaits the slightest attack. His outer demeanor of confident stoicism is an expression of who he wishes he could be and of who he sometimes convinces himself he is. In his worst moments, however, he's terrified that he's sub-standard and that everyone around him knows it but is lying about how wonderful they think he is. (An Aries will seldom keep anyone around who doesn't voice their positive opinion of him loudly and often.) This is when his critical nature rears its head and he starts to wallow in the past, accusing you of everything from lying about liking his shirt, to working your way through college as a prostitute. Ironically, these tirades and insults are geared at forcing you into a monologue about your deep loyalty and undying love for him. You are the glue that holds your relationship with him together, and he will test your strength. He wants a woman with greater loyalty than Juliet's, and he thinks that anything untested is innately weak. So he wars.

At his absolute best, his confidence is the stalwart of his life. He will make something out of himself, be successful, and take care of his family. He expects life to be difficult for everyone else and for the sake of philosophy, but he somehow never expects anything really bad to happen to him. Although he is given to a defeatist mentality when in a dark mood, he works very well under pressure.

In the sack, his confidence translates into sexual exuberance. As long as his fragile ego is catered to and he feels secure in your loyalty to him, he will worship you. He has no qualms about being naked, and is completely comfortable with your nudity. He *knows* that you will enjoy having sex with him many times a day.

He's an Idealist

The typical Aries started to define his perfect mate around the time he discovered that the mother he adored was not as perfect as he wished she had been. The truth hurt him and it can take an Aries years to recover—if he ever does. In the meantime, his mom taught him how to manipulate people, and the sharp disappointment he felt then encouraged his knee-jerk reaction to hurt anyone who hurts him. As a toddler pinches or bites the one who has taken his toy, so the Aries will name-call and blame with little regard for tact or respect.

In order to avoid such disappointment again, he will commit himself to finding the perfect woman—someone who is interesting, kind, loyal, submissive, and virginal. Unfortunately, the perfect woman doesn't exist, so Mr. Aries might create a cycle of disappointment in his life that reaffirms his distrust in women. After all, they continually betray his expectations. Some of these men spend their youths trying to find a real-life woman who comes close to how they envision their perfect mate to be. These Aries males don't know it yet, but they honestly wouldn't be able to handle their ideal woman—even if she existed—because she would accentuate their own inferiority and insecurities. They would run faster from her than from a lesser female. After repeated disappointment, an Aries tends to find a woman who is a blank slate: someone he can mold and fashion into what he wants her to be, someone he can dominate. But he'll never be happy with her because a servile woman can't give him the stimulus needed for the epic romance he craves. The truly happy Aries male learns to appreciate every woman for who she is and settles on keeping his ideal a wet dream without bringing too much resentment and heartache into his real-life relationships.

His idealism is a mixed blessing. It helps him achieve amazing feats in the bedroom as long as he's inspired and secure enough to trust his partner. It also helps him fall into a pit of despair at the slightest mistake or negative comment. As he ma-

9?8
4/84

tures, this too will change, and he'll learn to find harmony with his partner and to appreciate her for who she is and what she can do. He'll also have built up enough of a sexual history to feel confident in his abilities and be aware enough of his shortcomings to either compensate for them or hide them.

In his youth, he may have had difficulty accepting premarital sex as something that can be fulfilling and beautiful. His sex drive is strong enough to make him comfortable with the act (because he's aware of his drives and intentions) but he typically questions his partner's past and doubts her morality, which can lead to relationship problems. He may go so far as to lose respect for his partner immediately after sleeping with her. Even the most mature Aries is a follower of Courtly Love: the philosophy that a knight should dedicate himself completely to achieving the affection of someone who is emotionally and physically unavailable. Courtly Love is completely moral because, without any consummation following the achievement of respect and attention, the lady is seen as untouchable. Once the knight has been awarded a few brief moments in her presence, proof that her interest has been won, he moves on to another conquest. Similarly, an Aries puts a woman on a pedestal and the more he cannot have her the more desirable she becomes.

He's Dominant

Would you expect him to be any different? He's in control of every relationship, every conversation, every situation he's in. Even those times he says he's just along for the ride, he's in control of everything. He's surrounded with friends who look to him for some type of consolation or direction. He can be unable or unwilling to accept that others' opinions are as important as his own, even going so far as to believe that anyone who disagrees with him is either stupid, jealous, or evil. At his worst, he is a psychological abuser who swears that there's nothing wrong with him, only with you. At his best, he is more protective than a knight in shining armor, which is what he's always wanted to be. His dominance makes him a dynamic personality, capable of overcoming any obstacle.

He is the dominant one in bed. Even if he's tied spread-eagle to the bedposts, it will be in the guise of being worshiped rather than being controlled. And don't be surprised when he's worked himself out of the ties just to prove his dexterity and intelligence. To put it simply: the reason he's tied to the bed is so that you may pleasure him, not the other way around. He might play along with his lover's fantasies, but he prefers his sex based in reality, especially if that means he's co-starring in a passionate love affair with his perfect woman.

Just to get things straight, his perfect partner is not a subordinate one. The Aries male likes to be in control, but he loves a challenge. In a healthy sexual relationship, he feels free to express his masculinity and he revels in your submission. Any dominance on your part will have to have the air of deference. Some people call him selfish, others just admire that he knows his place in life.

Sex with an Aries Male

An Aries man has passion and *drive*. He loves sex, and in his youth he vacillated between needing it in his life and the moral implications of such an act. He wants to lose his mind in bed, to be completely entranced and involved without room for anything to intrude. As inviting as this sounds, it's hard to have sex with someone who expects perfection. Luckily, he can be very forgiving of physical imperfections, at least for a little while, even if he's much less forgiving with moral or character faults.

While the Aries male would like sex to remove all thought and hesitation from his mind, he gets into bed with his head first. He rarely has a one-night stand. If he does, he's driven as much by need as by revenge. He must love and respect someone to enter into a relationship with the person.

It's a fact that many of our insecurities are amplified in the bedroom, and Mr. Aries is no exception. His response to a per-ceived threat to his pride is quick (and sometimes cruel). On the other hand, he worships you in exchange for your unwavering adoration, and he's proud of his skill in bed. A youthful Aries expects women to vault into orgasm from his sheer closeness, and to be grateful for being in bed with him. If you're not, he'll be pissed. Thankfully, as he matures so does his sexual skill. He learns to understand women and appreciate the subtleties of sex. If it's hard to imagine why such a man's man would spend so much time refining his skill, remember that sex is all that poor Ares had to tie Aphrodite to him. The bed is where an Aries feels most like a man. There's never a question of who's in charge when you're being pounded by an enthusiastic Aries.

He doesn't seem to realize that all of his sexual desires re-volve around being dominant. Even if he acts submissively, it is with the air of a king granting a great boon to a lowly subject. Of course, he isn't the type to play a true Dom to any Sub. He could never respect a woman who submits to his every request, even if the idea interests him for the moment. He's instinctively aware that the Sub has the real power in that type of relationship, and he isn't keen on being the one with only the emblematic control of the Dom.

The Aries male is harder to please than almost any other man, and his mental games tend to exhaust his partners. One moment he wants a cloying virgin, and then he wants a seductive temptress with years of experience and tons of skill, and he wants sex on his terms—no matter what—even if his actions lessen his respect for you.

Lastly, he has a very good memory and he can be touchingly sentimental. He remembers how you felt beneath him, the flush of your cheeks, the musk of your sex, the feel of your nails digging into his back and driving him further in pain and ecstasy than he ever thought possible. He remembers, even though he may hate you for it.

Preferred Games

Heroic Knight Rescuing the Maiden

He loves to rescue women—absolutely loves it—and the more innocent she is, the more heroic he appears. He's not one who sees the beauty of Christ forgiving Mary Magdalene. On some level, Mr. Aries believes Christ should have withheld his mercy. His shaky ego loves the idea that his maiden has no one to compare him to, leaving him with nothing to worry about.

The Worshiped God

Oh, how he longs to be adored! In fact, he thought about it and he feels entitled to her worship. Now, it's an absolute requirement if she's with him. He wants to be pleasured, loved, and doted on. He needs the admiration of a more than willing partner if he is to play up fully to his masculinity. A word of advice: it will be worth your time to figure out how to make him worship you, too, because he's got the perfect pedestal to put the right woman on.

The Martyr

He will long after a woman he thinks is perfect for years, denying himself other women and suffering in his heartbreaking devotion to the unattainable one. This situation frees him from having to deal with reality and real women, and he quite possibly knows little to nothing about the actual object of his affection. The less he knows about her, the harder it will be for her to ruin his fantasy with any immoral or unfavorable action.

The John

He would love to screw someone without having to worry about her enjoyment or opinions. He wants to give orders and have them immediately carried out, to be the *customer* who must be satisfied. He revels in the dirtiness of prostitutes, but he'd never marry one. Sex is such a complicated matter for him, and he spends so much time thinking about his ideals and ethics that, for once, he wants sexual release without any complications.

Romeo

Every Aries man wants to be caught up in an epic romance with the partner of his dreams. The excitement and adventure of breaking rules, of making sacrifices for a lover and the sacrifices a lover makes for him, are the pinnacle of love and passion. He wants to be swept away from the everyday doldrums and taken to a world where love matters more than anything and devotion is proven time and time again without any doubts or second-guessing.

What He Needs to Learn About Sex

The Aries male needs to come to terms with imperfection, both his own and his partner's. He also needs to find out how to turn his ideals into a workable reality without feeling like he's "settling." Dreaming about an ideal partner when the day has been long and boring is one thing, but shunning a current lover in favor of a fantasy girl who'll never materialize is quite another. Mr. Aries needs to learn to love someone for their imperfections, not in spite of them. He also needs to reconcile sex and morality (or philosophy), depending on how religious he is.

What You Need to Know About
an *Aries* Woman

March 21–April 20

She wavers between total naiveté and being a fully bloomed woman. She entrances you with games of submission and dominance by taking control and then giving it up so whole-heartedly you know that you can do anything to her—anything at all—and she wouldn't protest. She is so far removed from any experience you've had before. Her passion is intoxicating and demanding, and yet tenderness remains. She nips at you, tears away clothes, moans as she straddles you and takes control, driving you both to utter madness. You love her and you know it. No one else could be like this; no one will ever be like this again. Then she feigns innocence and allows you to irrevocably corrupt her again and again, even going so far as to blush.

Goddess of War Incarnate

If you are unaware that Ares, god of war, is the ruling god of the warmongering Aries woman, you have either never met one or are in deep denial about what she's really like. An Aries woman lives to win, and will even make up little challenges throughout the day just to meet her quota of wars waged and won. While she may appear submissive, it's only a ploy, another weapon in her arsenal. She never backs down from a fight and cares not about the victims she leaves behind, thinking about them as often as a conquering Viking thinks about the villagers he's slain. And there have been and will be many victims. She exalts in power; it's the only thing in this world worth having because it *makes everything else possible*. Everything, that is, except love. The Aries woman may need a few years to figure that out.

The Aries female is more dynamic and energetic than her male counterpart. Where he hides behind a façade of idealism, she openly exerts her power and revels in it. Her anger and joy are usually open for everyone to see. Ares bestowed his longing for the ideal mate on his male disciple; to his female he gave his true heart. The Aries female has the strength to persevere and to stay loyal and devoted regardless of the challenges, even if it means staying in a bad relationship. While the male may be a strategizer, the female knows how to take action.

Frequently, the mind of an Aries woman turns to the dark, mysterious, and dangerous parts of life. She imagines her boyfriend's head suddenly exploding, or she thinks about her possible important role in the Apocalypse. You must keep in mind that Ares is not just the god of war, he's the god of brutal war, the god of making others suffer in as gory a way as possible. Thankfully, because of their need to gain power over everyone, Aries women are highly skilled actors. They appear as normal as possible, which helps them get their way. Only rarely do they call themselves Pestilence and jaunt around on white horses.

Her Top Traits Explored

She's Powerful

For good or ill, she's powerful. Actually, everyone is. The Aries woman will actually use her power, however, and with a vengeance. She knows how to get anyone to do whatever she wants them to do. She doesn't think twice about using others to her own advantage, and she feels no guilt for any problems she causes them. At most, she worries about how hard it will be to convince them to aid her again in the future.

While she knows how to get what she wants, tact is not her strong suit. She knows how to avoid pissing off someone, and when she has actually thought about someone else enough to form an opinion about them, she tends to just voice it without thinking or caring about the consequences.

The Aries woman can be a powerful ally or a dangerous enemy. Although she will take more crap from her lovers than from her friends, she applies the rules in much the same way for herself as for a lover. Some Aries women look for partners who are stronger and more masculine than they are. Others are more comfortable with a partner they can control. But, secretly, every Aries woman wants a man who can make her feel like a woman, and who isn't threatened by her independence and aggressiveness.

She knows exactly what she wants out of life, she's completely sure of her own value and abilities and willing to do whatever she needs to in order to get her way. Does she sound like a formidable partner? You have no idea. In bed she expresses herself through her body and passion. She isn't afraid to get dirty or to try something new, and her hungers are greater than those of the average succubus. When free of restricting doubts, she can make any man's wildest dreams come true, and it often turns out that sex holds her precarious relationships intact. The build-up and explosion of power that is the essence of an orgasm is an integral part of sex for her, and she's completely comfortable bringing herself to climax.

She's Eccentric

When you add impulsivity to an Aries woman's drive to do whatever she wants to do, whenever she wants to do it, you have one eccentric woman with high potential for becoming the crazy cat lady. And if love fails her too often, she'll have a closet full of guns later in life. She loves anything that's outside of the norm, and she really loves her ability to act on any impulse. She doesn't follow the usual path and she's a little unpredictable, which only underscores her importance and uniqueness. As she gets older, her eccentricity can harden, giving her a close-minded view of people and the world, and a belief that her way is the right way.

In addition to her eccentricity and in spite of her ferocity and independence, the Aries female is also very innocent, with a naïve view of herself and the world. Monsters under the bed are still very real to her when she's in her twenties, as are fairies and dragons. She's often unaware of others' intentions toward her, and she gets hurt when her naiveté cloaks her taste in men.

In her childhood, there was some trauma with sexuality, either molestation or extreme promiscuity. Because of her guileless attitude and how easily she can be hurt, she tends to inspire protectiveness in her male and female companions. The Aries woman feels entitled to protection, even if it gets in her way, and she's reluctant to give up her followers because they might prove useful later. Detachment and selfishness are large parts of her innocence. She simply doesn't know why she should care; and, like a baby, she only sees her own needs as important.

The Aries woman will improvise between the sheets, in the bathroom, or under the table to get her sexual needs gratified. She's a match for any man who dreams of a versatile lover with a desire as great as his own. She doesn't have a preconceived idea about what sex has to be like. Sex is an explosion of the senses for her; it's the most supreme exercise of her womanhood and power. She adores being adored, and she enjoys having power over a man.

She's Self-involved

The Aries woman is a selfish, powerful creature who doesn't follow anyone else's lead. She isn't confined to others' beliefs and her puerile innocence inoculates her against growing up. She doesn't understand anyone else's inner world or even believe there is a reason to try to understand it. The most important person to an Aries woman is herself.

An Aries often takes self-involved to extremes, which can definitely be annoying. However, knowing what she wants and needs can help her lead a more fulfilling and enriching life, and help to ensure that she's surrounded with people who will be there for her. This is the one trait that helps the naïve Aries weed negative people out of her life. She is more comfortable when others are just as selfish as she is because it reduces her need to worry about hurting them, and it gives her a definite role to play with little chance that her true self will ever be discovered.

She doesn't feel comfortable when her boyfriend hangs out with her friends, and for good reasons. First of all, her friends don't usually like him (they have numerous reasons); and secondly, she picks men who can do something for her, like spend money on her and satisfy her ego or sexual appetite. She doesn't look for a "buddy." She can have fun with her lovers, and even have good conversations with them, but she's never really their *friend*. The orgasm is such an emotional thing that it leaves her vulnerable to her partners. So, the less vulnerable she feels in other areas of the relationship, the more comfortable she will be.

Sex with an Aries Female

Very few, if any, women can please a man like the Aries woman can. She intuitively knows how to charm and excite her lovers and will go to any ends to make sure both she and her partner are fulfilled. She is capable of letting go of all inhibitions, and she genuinely loves sex, making her a bed partner many men would die for. She is a woman who seldom lets others into her own internal world. Instead, she reflects back at people what they want most to see in her. A protective male will see a delicate woman, a teacher will find an attentive and creative student, a friend will see a concerned confidante, and an enemy will see either a dangerous opponent or a submissive victim. The façade can last indefinitely, with the Aries woman having little desire to show her true self for fear that it will leave her vulnerable.

She is most attracted to partners who intimidate others, but who remain second-place to her. She's a competitive woman who is most gratified by finding a partner of equal or greater standing and then besting him throughout their relationship in both intellectual and emotional pursuits. She loves to prove to her lovers how impressive and unpredictable she is, as long as they aren't in a position to leave her or to easy to defeat. For this reason alone, she loves men with huge egos and long resumes. Because she's at her best and most vigorous when her love and passion have been aroused, her lovers will always mean more to her than any of her friends.

Despite her outer submissiveness, she's in charge of all of her relationships. She achieves her dominance through false subservience, flakiness, charm, stubbornness, and detachment from outcomes. Detachment curbs her vulnerability and once an Aries has felt pain she does her best to avoid it happening again. This can make forming actual relationships difficult for her, because in order to forge a true connection, she must risk being hurt. Because she's uncomfortable with true partnership, she tends to have little in common with her lovers. Sex is the glue that holds the relationship together.

The Aries woman, unlike others who expect their men to know how to get them off, is in full command of that department. She teaches her lovers how to be better in bed by sleeping with them and by being free with herself. She doesn't buy into the conservative view of sex. She's in it for pure pleasure.

Preferred Games

The Innocent Princess

The Aries woman can't be blamed for what she does, because her intentions are pure: to please herself. She's never lied to anyone about that fact, and her friends either accept her for who she is or leave. She loves to pretend that she doesn't know what she's doing, and it's true that sometimes she hasn't considered the possible repercussions for her actions, which exonerates her from them in her mind. The game allows her to sleep with whomever she wants, without any fault; to feel betrayed if she wanted sex to be more important than it was, and to avoid commitment if she doesn't have to have it. If anyone other than herself gets hurt, it's their fault because she never promised anything. Her intentions, after all, are pure.

The Queen of Flakiness

This game is a close alternative to the Innocent Princess, but it allows her to take commitment on her own terms. She can make or break a date, miss a phone call, or break "relationship rules" because she didn't understand them—or she forgot about them. She can't be held responsible for hurting anyone because her own needs come first and everyone around her understands that. She loves to pretend, but sometimes she's not pretending that she doesn't understand what other's expect of her. When that happens, she's sure not responsible for living up to it.

The Vixen Seductress

The Aries female believes that sex is power, and she loves to wield it over others. She will flaunt all of her skills to enchant a lover or else she becomes whatever he finds most seductive—be it a virgin, a heroine, a mother figure, or whatever. When she's seduced her lover into bed, she'll surprise him with her repertoire of skills, and she has a lot. There's enough sexual power in one Aries woman to satisfy half of the world, and to overwhelm anyone.

The Worshipped Goddess

Any man should feel privileged if an Aries woman has allowed him to be her lover, and he must treat her with the reverence she deserves. She loves the thought of having power over someone, and she enjoys being adored and feared. Her needs are the only ones worth considering, and her man should be thrilled enough just by her closeness, let alone any actual physical contact.

Wandering Lust

Whether in fantasy or reality, if her passion is not being quenched at home, the Aries woman will find someone else to put it out. If she's tired of a relationship or her beau has shown her that cheating is okay (what's good for the gander is good for the shotgun-wielding, cat-loving goose), she's likely to sample other men before breaking off her current engagement. She never really means to hurt anyone, so it's unlikely that anyone will ever find out about the indiscretion(s), but she's very concerned with getting what she wants and conventions aren't going to stop her. Besides, no one's ever been certain that a single man can handle all of an Aries woman's attention.

What She Needs to Learn About Sex

Sex can be the greatest union between two equal, loving partners, but in order to forge such a union, the Aries female needs to be willing to trust her lover, and allow him to see her for who she really is. She needs to cut the crap and start showing people her true self and try not to feel clingy, defensive, or needy afterwards. She also needs to drop the defense of being in control. There isn't always a winner or loser.

Taurus

What You Need to Know About
a *Taurus* Man

April 21–May 21

Blushing and stammering like the most inexperienced of men, the Taurus replaces the archetypal masculine approach to romance with an honest, down-to-earth attitude toward life and love and shy nervousness if you give him the chance. He cherishes you and delights in your touch, smell, and taste. He never takes your physical body for granted, despite how idiotic he may behave every once in a while. He's a man's man in the crowd, admired for his dignity and respectability. In your arms, though, he's tender as no one would expect this ambitious, suave man to be, and you love him for it.

Aphrodite, Goddess of Lust

Aphrodite, the Greeks' equivalent to the Romans' Venus, is the patroness of all Taurus people and of earthly pleasures. Aphrodite had the ability to submit to others outwardly while still doing whatever she wanted to do, and she gives the gift of outer submission to the Taurus male. The typical Taurus appears to never make major decisions and to either placidly go along with whatever is suggested by his mate or continue on the same path he's been on since high school. Aphrodite also makes him a slave to the senses, to acquisition, and to lust. His life is far less exciting than her adultery-filled life was, though.

Acceptance is little more than a comfortable façade for Mr. Taurus, just as it was for Aphrodite. However, Mr. Taurus uses it to escape accountability for any mistakes and to wriggle out of any uncomfortable chance-taking. Aphrodite was born an adult. The consequence for a Taurus of never having enjoyed a time when adventure reigned is an early and persistent maturity that is shadowed by a feeling of being entitled to act like a child well into adulthood. Both Aphrodite and Mr. Taurus insist on getting their way, no matter what anyone around them wants. They expect to be catered to, taken care of, admired, and adored regardless of how they treat others and what qualities they themselves possess. Even if the relationship is not sexual, the Taurus male will be surrounded by female admirers who depend on him for nurturing and support, just as Aphrodite herself loved to be encircled with devotees. However, just as with Aphrodite, the numerous female worshipers will be overseen by one authoritative force who will be the chief devotee and follower while still being wiser and more rational than Mr. Taurus himself. He needs a strong woman to rule his life

His Top Traits Explored

He's a Sensualist

This son of Aphrodite is a sucker for earthly pleasure. He loves good food, comfortable clothes, the way women smell, music, fuzzy animals, and sex. Although he isn't the most intellectual man, he definitely isn't stupid. He isn't an emotional guy either. He's a hedonist who relies on his senses to achieve pleasure and avoid every painful mistake he can. You see, when a Taurus gets hurt, it takes him a long time to recover, and he'll never forget or forgive himself, so he has to be careful about his decisions lest he cause a wound that will leave a horrendous scar. He's also sensitive to perceived slights and avoids socializing more out of fear of what people might think of him than of the people themselves. His love of sensual pleasures, staying at home, and his general hedonism make him prone to substance abuse and other overindulgences of the senses.

Mr. Taurus truly enjoys women. Most of his emotions are translated through touch and light jokes, and he's rarely up front about his feelings. He prefers to hold you all night long instead of entering into a diatribe about the way you and your smile make him want to cry, or that the smell of your hair haunts him throughout the day. At times it seems that only sex or great food can bring him out of his daily stupor.

In the bedroom, he delights in earthy, spicy smells such as nutmeg and cinnamon. He's driven crazy by caresses and the warmth of your skin. He appreciates your body and the joys it can bring to both of you. He isn't much for whispered vows of love, although he appreciates them. You're more likely to get them from him right before, during, or in the afterglow of sex than at any other time.

He's Possessive

No other sign is as inactive as a Taurus, and he can afford to be. It is a rare Taurus male who has not had his path set firmly before him since junior high. While he shows some definite ambition, he'd much rather sit back and let things come to him than go out searching for them. He knows what he wants, and mostly it's to be left in peace with his harem and queen. He lays out his plans and plots a course with such care that any sudden decisions or unexpected issue is highly uncomfortable—and Mr. Taurus enjoys his comfort.

Because his plans are so definite, his heart so easily broken, it takes a long time for him to learn to forgive his own mistakes. He's understandably obsessed with securing his belongings, and yes, you are one of them. He wants the most faithful wife, the biggest and most trustworthy car, the most energy efficient and comfortable house, and the securest job with as much upward mobility as possible. Those are his goals in life, with little variation, and once he has secured them, he can live in tranquility and with peace of mind about his eventual surrender to the unavoidable void. Unfortunately, this world is not always so simple, and while he's capable of dealing with many situations that arise, an unfaithful lover is not one of them.

He realizes how much of a chance he takes letting someone else into his life, someone with their own wants and needs, opinions and ideals. He hopes for the best, but his expressiveness is often curtailed by his fear that he will either be found unacceptable or that he won't be good enough. He sees infidelity as proof that he isn't good enough, that he's made a mistake in trusting you, and it breaks his heart whether or not you are aware of it. You may never know how possessive he is, but the intensity of his lovemaking after you've been checking out the cute new neighbor isn't just a mood he's in. If he loves you, he is honestly terrified of losing you, but he has no idea how to let you know that. Most of the time he just hopes you're as with him as he is with you.

He's Grounded

His feet are always flat on the floor. He's not one to kick up his heels without first determining that such a reaction is necessary. Of course he likes to have fun, but whatever merriment he partakes in must be practical. His relationships aren't based in hopes, fantasies, or idealisms. He understands his own and his partner's shortcomings. He is only willing to give his heart to a real partner, not some mythical woman based on boyhood dreams and *Play-*

boy. He plans his relationship with the frank honesty and strategy that he plans his finances. He does have a positive outlook, though, as his hedonism keeps him from dwelling on the inherent darker nature of humanity and the world. He has opinions and some of them may not be so Pollyannaish. While there may not be an actual silver lining, dark clouds don't tend to stick around for long. In his practical mind, the glass is neither half-full nor half-empty. It is refillable, as all glasses are. The amount is up to the holder, and he can never understand why so many foolish people ask themselves that age-old psychological-mindset-determining question anyway.

Sexually, he probably isn't going to dress up like a Roman emperor to pretend he's ravishing the pretty, innocent bath attendant. However, his preoccupation with the way things feel might have him venturing into some furry fantasies—anything that will produce more stimulation for his senses. But, in general, there's far too much enjoyment to be found simply in each other's body and all the incredible things those bodies can do. He's more attracted by touch than by intellectual games. He really likes sex anytime, although, he prefers the comfort of a bedroom and will need a little convincing before he accepts the notion of sex in a public restroom. Some Taurus males are more venturesome than others and all are apt to experiment sometime. Such exploration is more likely if Mr. Taurus is led by an aggressive partner with a sex drive as strong as her imagination. When the relationship is serious, he's a steady and loyal partner. If he's just out for some sex, he'll flop into one bed after another without looking back.

Sex with a Taurus Male

Sex with a Taurus is steeped in the senses. Every smell and touch is an augmentation for the act and not to be taken for granted. Aphrodite's influence gives him a need to be loved and taken care of and the ability to nurture the woman he's partnered with even if it's with a touch of selfishness. If his lover truly appreciates him, he'll bloom in the bedroom like he never will in a social setting, giving his partner the feeling that he is only himself when with her, but often leaving her in the role of protector and confidant. He adores her body, and he's proud of the way he can make her feel. If coupled with a detached intellectual, though, he'll wither under her sterile attentions and the relationship stands a good chance of ending because he needs to be needed. His ideal partner is a woman who is either as sensual as he or who knows how to cater to his senses by being a good cook, good lay, and good housekeeper.

He's a straightforward type of guy. His practicality imbues his every move, and he's nearly incapable of seeing beyond his own opinions of how the world works. Fortunately, he's good at business and finances, so his blindness doesn't generally stop him from having a successful career. It can make good relationships difficult, though. He wants a woman who will take care of him. He feels his debt is paid by being the financial support in return. He doesn't expect friendship or intellectual exercises. He's not comfortable being a bosom buddy to his wife or lover (he doesn't understand why she needs a close friend—he doesn't), and he doesn't know how to take care of someone emotionally, or even that someone would need their emotions looked after. He can be quite self-centered and even misogynistic in his beliefs about women and whether or not they have any value outside of the home. This, along with his possessiveness, can lead to his lover being cut off from her friends and social life. A Taurus doesn't need to be surrounded by friends to be happy, and as he ages, he prefers to be either alone with his partner or with his close-knit family.

Preferred Games

The Bread Winner

"He man, you woman. He kill animal, you cook, make baby. Ugh." Yep. He can be traditional-minded. His practical nature has forced him to confront the idea that men are different than women and that women are made to make babies and so on. He's the one who makes the big bucks and, in exchange, you owe him your care and gratitude, good food, and plenty of sex. This game works well for women who like their traditional role, but it can be a burden for everyone else.

The Little Boy

He likes being taken care of and he'll use whatever excuse he can to convince his partner that he's entitled to TLC 24/7. If being the breadwinner isn't good enough, he'll become the needy little boy who simply can't do anything without your help. You're his protector, mother, sex kitten, chauffeur, and chaperone. He'll act clueless and innocent, incapable or incompetent (never in a work setting, though) to make it more likely that you'll take good care of him. He'll do everything he can to get out of doing something he doesn't want to do, and his life's path was set long before you came into the picture.

The Hedonist

Aside from his famous willpower and solidarity, the Taurus is a slave to his senses and rarely finds any reason to take back the control they have over him. He enjoys feelings and will continue to seek that enjoyment, regardless of the consequences to himself or others. No, this doesn't mean he's a serial cheater, but it may have consequences in other parts of your relationship. If you want to have a successful relationship with this man, you need to remember that enjoyment and comfort are key, and the more of each, the happier he'll be.

The Ol' Come Hither

A Taurus male likes nothing better than to be taken care of by his woman. When it comes to sex, he loves a partner who is willing to take the initiative and do all of the work for him. He loves to be caressed, massaged, pampered, and teased. He doesn't expect to put out much effort to get sex. The more hoops someone makes him jump the less likely he is to take an interest.

The Gimmick

He's either the football star, the band member, the bad boy, or the gentleman. Whatever image he projects, he uses it to gain friends, to hide his true self behind, to get laid, and to fool others. He's much more comfortable being seen as an object (in the Simon de Beauvoir kind of way, not the Ayn Rand variety) than as a true individual with his own thoughts and feelings. He can function around people without much risk of being hurt if they see he has a purpose, that is, and as long as he keeps up his end of the bargain. He usually ends up with the person that everyone expected he will. For example, if he's the star athlete, he dates the cheerleader; if he's the number one employee, he either seeks out the number one in another division or he plays dirty with the secretary.

What He Needs to Learn About Sex

Taurus men need to learn how to sacrifice their comfort for the greater good. Some things in life are hard or unpleasant and sometimes the reward is small or not immediately noticeable. To sacrifice health or relationships because he doesn't want to give up some momentary comfort is ridiculous, though. His selfishness is reflected in all of his relationships, but it is brought to bear most heavily on his lover. He also needs to learn how to cater to his partner's needs and not to question whether or not those needs are practical or valid before doing even the smallest thing for her.

What You Need to Know About a *Taurus* Woman

April 21–May 21

The room is warm, the bed is comfortable and the air is full of her fragrance. She knows both exactly what you want and how to please herself without need to fumble and guess on your part. Eventually, you will learn her body as well as she seems to know yours. How she knows yours is a mystery, but one that you're thankful for as her exploring tongue reaches just the right spot on your thigh. Her eagerness is without guile. She offers herself to you without you knowing how much care went into the cost-benefit analysis of your third-quarter earnings and comparing how well you did last year to your prospects for the next year.

Aphrodite: Goddess of Lust, Beauty, and Pleasure

Aphrodite, at first glance, has little in common with the earthy Taurus woman. Whereas Aphrodite is vain, few could accuse the Taurus woman of being obsessed with her looks. Aphrodite had many affairs, but security-minded Taurus doesn't condone adultery. Fickle Aphrodite is not a reflection of the steadfast and true Taurus woman. It takes someone who knows the Taurus well to see what she might have in common with Aphrodite, and why it makes sense that such a down-to-earth girl is ruled by the wanton sex goddess.

Aphrodite loves herself above all others, and whatever pieces of her heart she gives away, it is more out of appreciation for her lover's infatuation with her than for any actual feeling for the man himself. The Taurus woman is not Aphrodite, though. They do, however, share some traits. They're both show callousness toward lovers and friends that hides an extremely sensitive heart and, like the goddess, the Taurus woman uses control and independence, along with feigned reliance on a lover, to ensure security and emotional safety.

Aphrodite loves to be admired and so does Ms. Taurus, even if her soft, playful demeanor makes her companions think that any admiration is an accidental byproduct of her personality rather than the result of long, drawn out, strategic plotting. Both the woman and the goddess expect admiration from others, and they can be petty and vindictive if it's not given. This preoccupation with social standing and dominance, when coupled with her materialism and lack of desire to explore the more ethereal aspects of life, can give both Aphrodite and the Taurus woman an air of immaturity. They may seem childlike in their delight with new things and people, or in the minor wars waged with other women who are competition.

Her Top Traits Explored

She's Warm

No other woman gives off the vibe of cuddly, happy, and motherly support like a Taurus female does. She is soft and strong, warm and snuggly, easy to hug, and hard to let go of. She truly loves her friends and family and she's willing to give so selflessly. She would make a good nun if only she were more religious and her practical mind allowed her to trust Catholicism more than the other thousands of religions, and then she'd have a doozy of a time trying to convince herself that she would be a worthy bride for the son of God. She's extremely protective and easily hurt. She's a joy when she's in love and a terror when she's in hate. Unlike her male counterpart, who seems to have the emotional spectrum of a bull, she feels everything so deeply it's a wonder that she can still smile and love as passionately as she does.

Like the Taurus male, she lives completely through her senses. She's more taken by an enticing aroma than an intellectual giant. Her chief purpose in life is to surround herself with comfort, not to divine the meaning of life or the best way to govern a society, and she shies away from anything unpleasant and refuses to sacrifice security for success. Relationships, in which her heart may be broken and her dreams tossed to the gutter by a mistaken alliance with a smooth talker, can be confusing and hard on her. She prefers her lovers to be more friend than Don Juan, and she won't jump into bed until she's sure she won't get hurt.

There's a word of caution about this side of her, though. However warm she appears to be, she may not stay that way unless carefully nurtured by loving hands. Her inner fire can turn to withering, detached strength, and her youthful buoyancy can vanish for good if her life is too difficult or if the love of her life has gone away either through tragedy or mischance. Once her heart is broken, it takes many years to heal.

She's in Control

So much of the Taurus woman's personality is made up of the need to find and sustain security that she can become obsessed with material things. Her natural optimism and warmth can fade, leaving behind a chilling emotional distance and a confining false wisdom that makes her want to let everyone else know exactly how they should be living their lives. The latter tendency can turn into a passion for helping others through organizations such as Alcoholics Anonymous or the Red Cross, however. At its worst, her need for security can drive her to pair up with unworthy partners and leave her in the role of caretaker, which sabotages any respect she has for her mate. This also makes it difficult for her to live up to her potential and fulfill her own dreams. As a final curse, she's born with natural accountability and she willingly shoulders the burdens of her mistakes. She stays in relationships far longer than she should and develops the habit of being unable to forgive herself for her mistakes. For as loving and caring as she is, the Taurus woman dances with a devil of a bitter end. She must learn to take the lead and save her inherent optimism or fall victim to its sterile beat.

In the bedroom her control is exerted in one of two ways: either by refusing to have sex with anyone but a serious partner, or refusing to get emotionally involved with her lover and using him as a tool to assuage her sexual needs. Her down-to-earth translation of Aphrodite's sexuality leaves her in love with the nitty-gritty, down-and-dirty part of sex. She has a huge sexual appetite and is usually one to explore all possibilities in the sex department.

She's Sensitive

Not many of her acquaintances are aware of the tentative hesitance with which the Taurus woman approaches relationships with others. She's loathe to give her trust to just anyone, and is always aware of how much someone can hurt her at any given moment. To prosper and be happy in life, she needs both physical and financial harmony and security from her mate. There is little use discussing her short-term affairs with men, for they are few, discreet, and generally meaningless once she's learned not to bring her heart into matters of the body. She's quick to size up a man's potential as a husband, and she won't stick around long for someone below par unless she's comfortable with physical closeness being the only kind of intimacy they share and is assured of the discretion and respect of her partner. She's very sensitive to any slights, and always aware of her standing with others. Despite being harsh with herself and her smarter-than-thou attitude, she easily accepts and forgives (but never forgets) others' flaws. She finds it difficult to hold them close afterwards, though. Her sensitivity to others gives her a natural ability to psychoanalyze, and she is a skilled, if not warm, counselor to her friends and loved ones. She gets haughty, however, if her advice is rejected.

Her sensitivity is the root of her good taste and the core of her success. She's hypersensitive to the relationships, strengths, and weaknesses of the people she encounters and knows instinctively how to get what she wants from just about anyone. Because it is so easy, though, she usually outgrows the habit before her twenties, preferring instead to live her own life and to let others live theirs. This, of course, doesn't apply to her husband, because his life is a reflection of her own and he must live up to her ideals.

As long as she's happy, she uses her knowledge of what people want, which is an advantage to her partner because she caters to his needs before he can make requests. The other side of the sensitive coin is that she's very open to negative vibes, implied insults, or general disapproval. She resents being judged, no matter how often she judges others. If she's upset, sex with her is like chiseling into a stone with no artistic inclination. Eventually, you'll ruin it.

Sex with a Taurus Female

The Taurus woman is about as sensual as a woman can get. She honestly loves sex and adores being touched and held, even if she sometimes seems to recoil from close contact. It is because of her extreme sensitivity to it. If she trusts her partner, or is in the mood for an illicit affair, she can bring such skill to the bedroom that her lover is confused about what happened to the quiet and self-contained woman he brought home. She has a definite exhibitionist streak, and she gets excited by the possibility of discovery, or by the knowledge that others can see or hear her having sex. She's aware of how powerful sex can be, and is ultra-sensitive about her attractive friends. She's constantly comparing herself to them. Sometimes this comparison can lead her into lesbianism if she mistakes intense jealousy and her need to be seen as a sexual powerhouse for lust.

She is always the leader. It doesn't matter who made the initial advance, who's on top, or who sneaks out before the light of dawn, the Taurus woman is in complete control of the situation. Even in the rare moments when she makes a mistake, she'll shoulder the blame with the solemnity of a martyr. She's an imposing woman, a threat to insecure men, someone who can overshadow every aspect of a partner's life for better or for worse. Her confidence, solemnity, warmth, and skill give her the air of someone who's in charge, and she'd better stay in charge for the sake of everyone around her. Not to say a partner can't live his own life—she'll adopt his dreams with gusto if she's in love. She's an involved girlfriend or wife, though, and many men are content to let her be so.

Everything about this woman is physically satisfying. She's a phenomenal cook (or else she's got good enough taste to order from great restaurants), an outstanding lover, and a supportive partner. She's even got a certain skill with conversation. She's extremely sensual, and blooms when all of her senses are comforted with pleasant smells, tastes, sights, and touches. Even if the world has been hard on her, and she's developed a thick skin and a morose countenance, she's still far more sensitive than she lets on.

Preferred Games

The Little Wife

She'll cook, clean, fold the laundry, and delight in all of the housewife's tasks, even if she's known you for only a week. As time goes by, the novelty diminishes and the "little wife's" independent streak, which is the size of the Grand Canyon, returns. She won't stop being wifely, but her duties will switch. She'll strengthen your business proposal instead of washing dishes, and she'll design the graphics for your presentation on Friday instead of baking the perfect soufflé.

Woman with a Cause

Every Taurus woman has a cause she champions—the blind, the homeless, Al-Anon—anything that lets her help others find the security and help they've been deprived of through legal disenfranchisement, lack of self-discipline, tragedy, and so forth. These causes help her heal her own wounds and those in her relationships. She'll never stop her humanitarian efforts, and that alone says how easily and deeply she's hurt herself.

Just a Little Odd

She has a wild streak. There is a part of her that delights in the bizarre and macabre. When she's in love with herself (always a good state for a Taurus to be in) she gets so much joy and release from following her own inclinations that it's almost sinful to contain or reprimand her. Her partner must be careful to do neither, especially when sex is involved. She proves that loving yourself is the first step in loving others and being happy with your life.

Classy

She has an air of self-possession and grace that makes others wonder what secrets of life she holds that make her so calm. Her movements and speech are careful and deliberate, especially when she's trying to impress. This tendency to be concerned about how she appears and what others think about her diminishes somewhat as she matures. She's old-fashioned in her opinions about sex and is the type of girl who brings out the best in men in the bedroom—at least in the beginning of the relationship.

Hedonistic

She lives for physical pleasure. She loves good food, art, music, textures, and smells; and she revels in the close contact sport of sex. She has trouble staying away from something that feels so good and has difficulty reconciling it with its possibly negative repercussions. She's also prone to substance abuse and overindulgence with food and alcohol.

What She Needs to Learn About Sex

Vulnerability does not necessarily mean weakness, and showing it does not automatically lead to degradation. She does not need to turn herself into a woman who takes sex lightly just because that's the trend in society, nor does she need to abstain for fear of her reputation. Ms. Taurus needs to discover what honor means to her and decide how she can best live up to her own expectations.

Gemini

What You Need to Know About a *Gemini* Man

May 22–June 21

The silence is broken by the steady slap of leather on skin and the sound of air unwillingly escaping from clenched teeth. The candles' glow reflected in his eyes adds to the intensity of his gaze as he looks at you lying before him. There is no love or passion, only purpose and intent. In some way, each of you has ceased to be unique, conscious, and intellectual beings, and instead have become nothing more than a collection of nerve endings that exist for no other reason than to feel and to be felt. But you know that at any moment one of you might laugh and the tenuous hold of this rare focus will break. It won't even be missed.

Mercury, God of Used Car Salesmen

Enough said. Mercury, messenger of the gods on Mt. Olympus, god of Gemini and of the man he governs, is sly and quick-tongued—a used car salesmen who changes easily from cloying to sarcastic. He charms, insists, and promises the moon. Then he delivers a hunk of Swiss cheese with a doctoral dissertation on their philosophical similarities.

They're always on the move, flirtatious, a man's man (although no man alive really ever trusts any of them), and their true and hilarious character is an infuriating scoundrel, a forced extrovert who'd rather be curled up with a good book and a vibrant lover. Only half of him is aware of the path he travels. Mercury is known to lead souls to the afterlife and to bring dreams to the sleeping. The Gemini male can neither escape daydreaming nor pledge himself fully to realism. Mercury's mind and the myths that surround him are indicative of a god who never stands still for long, and who, although he delivers messages, is only connected to reality through his silver tongue and quick feet.

Mercury gave his favored son, the Gemini male, a tactful and solicitous tongue and adorned him with the frank mannerisms of someone who is honest so as to convince others of his integrity.

Whether or not he is in fact acting with integrity is something of which neither the god nor the man is sure. After all, the best liars are the ones who know not that they're lying. Because he is such a political god, it's hard to understand who the real Mercury is. The same is true for the Gemini male.

His Top Traits Explored

He's a Dreamer

A Gemini man spends most of his time in his head, daydreaming and plotting, but in reality he does little to change or progress unless ruthlessly prodded by someone he loves and respects. A relationship with him is seldom what anyone thinks it is, and that's why some of the things he does and says can be so unexpected and come across so strange. Every woman in love with a Gemini wonders, at some point, if her heart belongs to a paranoid schizophrenic, and she's got reason to worry because the Gemini's reality is not the same reality the rest of us know. And there's usually at least two of him.

He loves with the devotion of a drugged man, swearing undying oaths and allegiance while being semi-aware that the worshipful state he's in could crumble and disappear with as little significance as a puff of smoke, not even leaving the memory of what it had once been. He needs a woman who will change with his dreams: it's an illusive dream with enough, and no more, substance than that needed to caress, thrust into, and intoxicate him. He needs one hell of a confident woman who isn't threatened by his changing ideals, bad memory, and long list of forgotten lovers. His dreams often find their way into the bedroom, and Mr. Gemini is an imaginative lover who will try anything. Yet, he's completely satisfied with the bare minimum as long as his partner is attractive, or he's desperate or in love.

He's Charismatic

There are few people who can dislike a Gemini when he's at his most charming. He's so naturally buoyant and positive, charming and likable, that it takes someone who knows him well to want to see him smothered in his sleep. At first, people aren't aware that his charm is based on his dreamy nature, and that half of everything he says is a "mistaken memory"—also known as a lie. But still, there's enough good in him that most can easily forgive his "mistakes." As he matures, he will either make fewer mistakes, or he'll grow more skilled in making mistakes so others find it nearly impossible to perceive he made one at all. (Note that a Gemini's maturity is not based on chronological age but rather on when he decides to accept the real world and his place within it.)

One outlet of his charisma that tends to infuriate his less confident (and even some very confident) partners is his flirtatious attitude. He could have one eye, a club foot, and look like he hasn't taken a bath in months (Geminis always smell good, regardless of how they look), and he can still make the most uptight woman giggle like a gay man backstage at *WWE Raw*. Those women who aren't jealous types will be grateful for the doors Mr. Gemini can open with his charm. For those who see green whenever another woman even glances his way, well, good luck to them.

He's a charming and forgiving lover who's seriously concerned about pleasing his partner. He likes variety, but is thrilled with sentimentality as well. He craves a versatile and dominant partner who'll bring out the male inside him, which sometimes he feels isn't really there. It's part of always being dual-natured— he's never quite sure what his other side looks like.

He's a Sponge

This man soaks up whatever is going on around him. If his partner is moody and depressed, he's likely to become unstable and unhappy. If his partner is ambitious, he's pushing ahead. If she's political, he's running for mayor. If she's paranoid, he's hiding in the bushes with a shotgun. It doesn't matter that he's only half playing along with her, because he's only half playing along with being a member of the human species, too. His disbelief in reality is so much that he's only half sure he has a penis between his legs when all he really needs to do is reach down and give the thing a jiggle to convince himself it's there. But *oh no*, Mr. Gemini could never support any of his conclusions on something *too* obvious.

That sponginess is behind all of his personality traits; it's how he makes friends, and it's the basis of his charm. He's collected so much random knowledge and experience that he can relate to just about anyone at anytime. It's what leads him on his many adventures and what usually leads him astray. He's convinced that the grass must be greener on the other side of whatever. He has a childlike acceptance of what others tell him, and whoever he's around the most has the most influence on who he is at the moment. Once a relationship ends, it doesn't take long for him to be nothing like he was when the relationship was going on, which confuses his exes and scares his current partner. She knows there's no real way to tell if the new relationship is more important or stable to him than the last one was.

Sex with a Gemini Male

Despite his healthy sex drive, the Gemini lives in his head full-time. He approaches eroticism from an intellectual point of view and appreciates the *feel* of sex, although, he's not passionate about it and doesn't need it to survive. It's his detachment from sex that pushes him to try new ways of having it, and urges him to contort his body into the most unimaginable positions just because his partner asked him to, or one of his friends told him he should try it.

The Gemini male is the true bad boy with the heart of gold —a good girl's dream come true. Not that he's really bad. He's just detached and curious and unaware of the effect his actions have on others. He tries so hard to be good, and he knows all of the right things to say and how to relate to a woman and it's almost impossible to be angry with him for long. He's an irresistible challenge so that getting him to stay settled down takes constant vigilance and strategizing. Almost any woman could make him work for her love, but only a skilled one will keep him working.

The Gemini male wants to be dominated in every aspect of his life. He wants to be seduced, cajoled, persuaded, and cared for by his lovers. He hates being tied down by physical concerns and prefers his food and money to magically appear before him without any effort or worry from him. Ironically, he loves to feel like the protector and breadwinner, and few things make him happier than working with his hands and creating. When he was younger, he always had to force himself to commit to things and that led him to committing to the wrong woman more than once. Because of this, he tends to be part of incredibly poor relationships where the woman is weaker and needier than he (so he can protect her), and yet demanding and unsatisfied (because he only likes dominant women). Both of them tend to be miserable. It's only when he discovers his boundaries and needs that solid partnerships are possible.

Preferred Games

The Gymnastic Instructor

At first he seemed kinky, but now you know he's just grieving over the Stretch Armstrong doll he lost when he was a kid. He likes nothing more than seeing what positions he can get into with a partner. Twister would be a relaxing diversion after a tryst with Mr. Gemini. Eventually, though, sex becomes only a game and it's not even about kinkiness anymore.

The Protector

He's always felt a little out of control, and challenged to handle his own changeable nature. He wants to be in charge of something and to do a good job of it, but he's not always willing to put out much effort. The easy victory suits him best and satisfies him least. He loves to be in a position of power during sex, as if he's desperate to save his lover from someone (it doesn't matter if that someone is himself).

The Objective

His inability to get out of his head and his fascination with the act of sex make it nearly impossible for him to ever really make love. The passion simply isn't there. He can appreciate his partner, but never meld with her. He feels her body, but he doesn't know how to savor it. After the initial excitement, sex becomes a means to an end, and his partner little more than the vessel to transmit it.

Drama Queen

Nobody loves being surrounded by drama more than the Gemini male. Oh, he might scream for peace, but he'd never just ask for it. He isn't jealous and there aren't many emotions that touch his core, but drama enchants his mind and soul, and while he supposedly hates it, he clamors for more. It makes sex interesting, it gives a false sense of passion to the relationship, it gives him an excuse not to try harder to succeed, and it's his scapegoat for everything. As he matures, he might be able to turn his need for drama into a passion or an ambition, but until then . . .

The Consummate Good Guy

He'd twist his testicles into knots if it meant being a better lover. By the time he's in his twenties, he's used to being stepped on by the women he loves, and he hasn't yet reached the decision to set up boundaries. Because he expects to be trampled, he draws women to himself who are diehard tramplers and it takes a huge leap of faith to wait for something better.

What He Needs to Learn About Sex

Mr. Gemini needs to learn to focus on one thing at a time and to mesh his inner fantasy life with outer reality without being too pessimistic. Learning how to stand on his own two feet without using a partner to prop him up would do him some good as well. It would also allow him to take further steps into reality. Sex isn't about codependence; it isn't only about the physical sensations, either.

What You Need to Know About
a *Gemini* Woman

May 22–June 21

You thought she'd be offended when you recommended she do something with her mouth other than chatter away while you're trying to arouse her. Surprisingly, your suggestion seemed to do the trick and focused her mind and her mouth on the business at hand. She always surprises you in these little ways, and you're grateful to have found a partner who never bores you, even if you're a little nervous about keeping her attention for any length of time. Friendship, gratitude, and surprise are three of the cornerstones to your relationship, but you can't seem to find the fourth no matter how hard you look for it, and it's absence is really starting to trouble you.

Mercury, God of Used Car Salesmen

Always more aware and knowledgeable than the gods to whom he gives messages, Mercury carries a vast store of knowledge between his ears, and uses it to his best advantage. Clever, quick-tongued, and manipulative, he plays up his innocence and trustworthiness while undermining his friends and opponents alike with such charm and cunning that they rarely get angry with him—if they even figure out what he's up to. While the Gemini woman is seldom ambitious enough to use her talents excessively, she's a collector of people and information, and she isn't always the most selfless person in the room. She, like Mercury, enjoys mental games, intellectual superiority, and answering to no one else, regardless of whom they call master at the moment.

Besides being duplicitous and insensitive, Mercury is also the god of thievery. When just a baby, he stole cattle that belonged to his half brothers for the fun of it and to assuage his need to deceive those who egotistically thought they were smarter than him. The Gemini woman enjoys playing with people's assumptions, too, and she can easily convince herself that anything she does is moral and right because the people she has done it to had it coming. Of course, she doesn't need to convince herself for long, because five minutes after the act is committed she considers it ancient history. Nothing thrills her more than doing something unexpected and watching the reactions of those around her. While she can melt into the background, she enjoys being the center of intrigue and speculation. As with her patron Mercury, the Gemini female uses her wit as both a weapon and to placate others. While she's generally well-liked, no one really knows the woman behind the façade that she will never drop.

Her Top Traits Explored

She's the Belle of the Ball

While she's not exactly what some consider vain or self-centered, the Gemini woman loves being the center of attention. She loves entertaining and pleasing others, she lives for flirting, and she can't stop herself from using her wit—even if it's at the expense of someone else's feelings. She wants to be wanted and admired, and she's charming enough to persuade anyone who doesn't know her well to fall in love with her.

More than anything, she wants people to think that she's *interesting*. She cultivates hobbies and gathers information to delight others and to prove how eclectic and intelligent she is. She is easily bored, and no one is as dangerous as a bored Gemini. She can topple towns, destroy reputations and relationships, and disassemble the plasma screen television to see how it works (and with no idea either of how to fix it or how to pay for a new one). She needs to be doing something and any lull in activity will have her anxiety and blood pressure rising.

In the bedroom, her entertaining abilities fall somewhat short of her promises. She's more intellectual than physical, and the act of sex tends to bore her unless there's an interesting conversation occurring at the same time as coitus. Her lover must capture her imagination.

For a woman who wants the greatest amount of stimulus at all times, the chase is inevitably more interesting and dramatic than the capture. If you have your eye on more than just a fling, you'd better know how to play a smooth game of cat and mouse, and be prepared to keep it going until you decide to part ways with the Gemini.

She's Stimulating

Everything in her life is about the give and take of human interaction. She enjoys anything that has to do with how two or more subjects interact, including politics, psychology, or education, etc.

She especially enjoys being in a position of knowledge and power when she deals with those subjects. Even if she isn't particularly interested in a subject, if it's popular with her friends, she'll learn everything about it she can in order to converse with them and keep up her reputation of being "in the know."

She's charming and vivacious. She knows the best complements and comebacks, and she's your best friend. She's unlikely to stick around for long, though, if things become too emotionally draining. She's charming to the extreme, which is part of her ability to stimulate others to see her point of view or to feel toward her the way she wants them to, and she's an expert at inciting both friendships and hatreds, depending on her inclination at the time.

She's Solitary

Not quite independent, but solitary, she experiences the loneliness of a person who has known her other half intimately, and has lost it somewhere. She has trouble reconciling that no one else will ever know who she really is and that few will ever be more than an acquaintance. She compensates by having a colorful inner life. She's best when operating on her own, even if she's terrified of being alone. She loves being around people and seeing herself played off of them, but she'll never be comfortable with a truly intimate connection. She uses her intellect as a way to form connections and to keep those connections from becoming too emotional, but her motives, her thoughts, and her intent will always be somewhat of a mystery. Count yourself lucky if you know even a third of her actions.

A Gemini woman is dreamy, somewhat flaky, and never too sure of what reality is. She lives in her head and the relationship you have with her isn't necessarily the same one you think you're in. You can never be too sure if she's in love with the real you or the you she imagines you to be. But, then again, that is true of many people and many relationships. When dating a Gemini woman, you must understand that her chief motivator is to escape from boredom. She requires constant entertainment and change in order to be happy. Some of her best relationships are with men who share her hobbies, and who are almost as changeable as she is.

You might think that sex with such an unpredictable woman would be exciting, and if she's in the right mood, it will be. But the act of sex is so routine, so utterly predictable—it always has a bunch of thrusting and the same end over and over—that she's not very interested in it. Instead, the Gemini woman barters, using sex as a means of payment for your conversation and partnership. She may convince herself that sexuality is beautiful and meaningful (because that has been the trendy way of thinking about sex since the sixties). Whether or not she actually believes it is more up to the skills of her partner, his intelligence, and the fantasies she has than to any generalized opinion on her part.

Sex with a Gemini Female

When she's into it, she's *really* into it, but when she's distracted or bored, forget it. The Gemini woman needs a partner who intrigues her, who can keep up with her mental games and stand up to her ideals, and who isn't going to back down when she goes a little crazy, which all Geminis admit to doing now and then. With a willing partner, she's more than happy to play sexual games and get into some kinky scenes—anything to avoid boredom. She loves innovation and change, and her partner will either change with her or be left behind. The Gemini woman has a lot of preconceived ideas about what sex with her perfect partner will be like. She has an opinion about what sex should be like, who she should have it with, and what the relationship will be like when she does have it. Sure, she'll go through periods of promiscuity and born-again virginity, but she'll always have a strong belief behind why she's doing any of it. There's no one like a Gemini when it comes to giving excuses or explanations. She isn't bound by the truth, so some of her reasoning can get pretty inventive.

She's energetic in the bedroom, and if she ever just lies there and takes what you dish out without any ideas or excitement of her own, you have a huge problem on your hands. If she isn't responsive during sex, then her mind is somewhere else because she's bored, and wherever her mind is, her body will soon follow. With a Gemini woman, always tackle her mind before anything else. She's bored by quiet, soft-spoken, or just plain stupid men, but part of her is intrigued by silent types. She needs to be with someone who understands the way her flighty mind works and who knows the perfect way to keep her softly grounded while also letting her fly every now and then. A mature and happy Gemini woman eventually comes to understand that she must find companionship and confidence within herself before she can accept it from anyone else.

She's got enough idealism and ardor to bring out the best in any man. She's a lovely instructor in the art of love and can easily take someone from their first kiss to their first homemade porn. Although she loves to pretend that she's completely uninhibited (she's willing to get down and dirty), she's actually quite sensitive and prefers sweet nothings to calling her boyfriend "daddy" and begging for a spanking. Even if whips and chains don't make her blush, being treated like a brainless object or being put into the role of one will make her leave, even if she has a tendency to objectify others herself.

Preferred Games

The Prima Donna

Every Gemini woman longs for the perfect audience. She wants to be admired and watched by her lovers, to be seen as almost within reach and utterly desirable. Although she isn't necessarily looking for a co-star, a part of her is starving for one. After such a long time of being alone, though, she'll settle for what she can get, which is a pleased spectator. She loves to hear herself talk. She's thrilled by the thought of what her lover is thinking about her, and she plays to his reactions.

The Caregiver

When in doubt about her own needs and her ability to satisfy them, and as a way to escape her own loneliness and emotional isolation, the Gemini woman strives to become an integral part in the lives of the people around her. A lost Gemini will often devote herself to volunteer work, hoping to flesh out some of the meaning of her life, and she tends to become involved with needy and manipulative partners.

The Unrepentant Vamp

She's a hard-core flirt who loves the excitement of the chase, even if she has no intention of seeing it through to the end. She adores having men chasing after her and seeing women jealous. At her most coquettish, she believes she can get any man she desires into bed, and she will make much effort to prove it to herself and to her victim's wife or girlfriend.

Queen of the Fifth Dimension

She's rarely here with the rest of us. Most of the time this Gemini woman is lost in fantasies, and the more disparity between her dreams and her reality the less inclined she is to keep buying that return ticket from her mental vacations. She may get to the point where she's more in love with the lover in her head than with the one beside her in bed at night. When her lover continually fails to live up to her expectations, she digs out the chasm between them even wider.

Jealous Much?

The Gemini woman loves men. She needs variety in her sex life, and unless she's spent much time learning about all the ways one can have sex, she translates "variety" into "as many men as possible." Even when involved, she keeps a group of male friends close, just in case she starts feeling lonely or begins to think her man is taking her for granted. Instead of being open about any insecurities, she prefers to make her lovers work for her attention, and she enjoys watching them vie for it with other potential suitors.

What She Needs to Learn About Sex

The Gemini woman needs to learn to accept the reality of both situations and people. While she feels an aching need to find her lost twin, she cannot blame others for not living up to her expectations. She needs to realize that part of this search for her other half is an attempt to block herself from being honestly vulnerable with her mate and to come to terms with what life really is, without all the fantasies.

Cancer

What You Need to Know About
a *Cancer* Man

June 22– July 22

There is never so much care in all the world as there is in this man's touch. It is not the care of a man afraid to break you, but of a man blissfully in love with your body. The proximity it has to reverence startles you and you feel the responsibility of his sensitivity weigh on your shoulders, neither heavy nor light, but a definite presence. No matter how many others he has been with, there is no doubt that you are the one that matters. His caresses, his nibbles, his delight in your response melt you and you become like chocolate on his velvet tongue.

Prince of Swiss Cheese

In many cultures, the moon is seen as the embodiment of femininity. The waxing, waning, and full moons are seen at the beginning, end, and pinnacle of life; and the moon herself is considered to be a primary symbol of the Mother. Being a male who belongs to a patron so steeped in femininity gives the Cancer man an unusual sensitivity to women and their needs, and a deep connection to and knowledge of his own emotions and the emotions of others. The problem with his sensitivity, however, is that he doesn't discriminate between being everything his partner wants and everything every woman in the room wants. He gallantly flirts and comforts everyone around, often mistaking companionable closeness for romantic feeling.

While female Cancers seem to embrace their femininity and are able to channel their strengths into successes, Cancer males are consumed by it and are either destroyed or hardened under the moon's cold light. Ever aware of his deeply feminine nature, he seeks to adorn himself outwardly with everything he needs to convince himself and the rest of us that he's "one of the boys." He seeks wealth, an admirable career, and the perfect woman to keep his home happy and his friends jealous. However, there is a dark side to the moon, and while she shows us one face, there is another that we will never see. The Cancer, too, hides his inner nature and only rarely accomplishes what he professes to others are his goals. Cancer men will always live a secret life and be a mystery to others. If he one day appears to be as affable as the man on the moon, the next his story is as full of holes as Swiss cheese.

His Top Traits Explored

He's Sensitive

Did I just hear a universal groan? I'm sure, if you are one or know of one, you've read in many astrology books how sensitive the Cancer is. There's a reason why every astrology book underlines this trait—because it's his chief one. It dictates what all of his other traits will be, it's what makes him love and hate, and it's what propels him into his career and friendships. Without sensitivity, the Cancer man would not be who he is. He'd have no reason to maintain that Crab shell.

The Cancer male's sensitivity, which can be attributed to his intuitive nature, helps to raise his awareness of the inner workings of his close associates and lovers. One of the reasons why so many Cancer men are single is because of their reluctance to form a close attachment with someone whose moods and fears would infiltrate his closely guarded and maintained world. He isn't the oblivious "manly" man type who forgets your anniversary and birthday, or who is unaffected by your tears and laughter. In fact, long after the relationship is over, he'll still shed a tear or two himself when the clock strikes the exact hour the two of you met. When he's at his best, he can intuit your sexual and emotional needs. The problem with being so emotionally in tune with so many women at one time is that there's a large chance he'll become too involved as a friend's caretaker and will end up straying sexually and emotionally from his main relationship.

Another part of his sensitivity is his sweetness. He's a romantic, attentive, demonstrative, and devoted partner. He demands loyalty and stability because all of his attentions put him at great emotional risk. A Cancer man who is either inexperienced in love or jaded by it can allow his defenses to take over and control his relationships, in which case his intuition becomes a weapon to destroy his natural sweetness and the woman he's with.

He's Emotional

The Cancer man is not afraid to cry, and he usually looks heart-breakingly beautiful when he does. When he's in love, he feels it in every pore, and when he's upset, his whole body tingles with adrenalin and frustration. Not that you'd ever know it, because while he won't hesitate to cry or laugh, his deeper emotions take some prodding before they come to the surface. He must feel secure before he'll let anyone else know about them.

Most of this man's actions are based on emotions—emotions that are seldom rational and which have a tendency of standing as false witness for his defenses. If he's had a happy life, full of friends and family, he's probably very likable and suave, and his bad moods will be less noticeable than those of a Cancer whose shell has hardened from frequent mistrust and humiliation. Either way, he's likely surrounded with a misty air rather than a piercingly realistic view of the world. All corners are rounded in the Cancer's world, and he functions better if it's carpeted as well.

Once he's stabilized and he feels secure with himself and his lover, sex becomes a joyous and explosive act of union between two blissful partners. However, if there are sexual problems in the relationship, rather than confronting them with his usual insight, he'll see them as a sign of a problem within himself and staunchly avoid discussing them whenever possible, turning a fissure into the Grand Canyon in record time.

He's Self-involved

There isn't much that the Cancer cares about beyond his own wants and needs, security and comfort. He isn't interested in world peace and, despite his many humanitarian efforts within his small circle of friends, he doesn't care that much about what others are going through. Most of the time he's certain that they bring it on themselves and he enjoys watching them suffer the consequences. Being so self-involved is one of his main defenses, and this boy has *a lot* of defenses. Having so much intuitive information about how others feel necessitates closing himself off from the rest of the world unless he becomes so overwhelmed that he can't function. For his own security, he limits the scope of cares and concerns and shields himself with self-aggrandizements and critiques of others. Security is the chief concern of a man who is so thin-skinned that the smallest slight penetrates him.

In order to keep from caring too much about what occurs in a relationship, you can expect him to always keep some distance, even though he'll probably appear charming and accommodating throughout. He's afraid of being hurt, and will only let others know how deeply he feels when he's certain that he won't be rejected or humiliated. He understands what he wants from the relationship and goes after it with total focus and much disregard for everything else, even putting his insights about what *you* want to the wayside at times.

His goal in life is to fulfill his own desires. Count on him to be into sex for his own pleasure. He'll be mildly proud if you get anything out of the experience, and there are a few Cancer men out there who have learned the joy of pleasing a woman before themselves, but these are few and far between.

Sex with a Cancer Male

He's the perfect man for those of you who like tender, dreamy sex with a man who swoons every time he looks into your love-filled eyes. He's masculine and fragile at the same time, which is why so many Cancer men enjoy wearing makeup and dressing provocatively; it gives them a chance to look pretty and an excuse to fight all at once. He is mostly attracted to strong, opinionated women who come ready-made with their own cartload of friends and followers. He has a history of dating the same type of woman and dealing with the same type of problems over and over until something explosive happens to knock him out of the cycle.

He absolutely adores being friends with women. If it were up to him, and if women weren't so neurotically emotional and irrational (or so his defenses tell him), he'd be *surrounded* by women—positively unable to breathe or think without smelling their musk or hearing their tinkling laughter. He loves to hold them when they cry, he shivers with anticipation of rescuing them from ungrateful boyfriends or husbands, of being the one man in all the world who treats them with the reverence they deserve. He's also the one who slams them to the metaphorical ground with the thunderous force of his I-told-you-so's and I'm-better-than's, depending on his own emotional well-being at the moment. He's the type of guy whose friendships with women will always be a threat to his romantic relationships, but who will never be willing to leave his friends behind.

He isn't that into sexual games or role playing as he believes in the simplicity of nakedness and sex. In his regular life, he may enjoy wearing costumes, and there's always an air of the artist around him. This often leads him to act in whatever way he thinks an artist should, either drinking and drugs or the life of a troubled hermit, but his sexual appetite is rather perfunctory. He'd enjoy a change of position or setting rather than a change of personality, as the latter threatens his stability in his relationship and his comfort with his partner. He enjoys looking good, and being with a partner who looks good, and his friendships with women ensure that he's typically paired with a woman who's better looking and more accomplished than he is himself.

Preferred Games

The Buddy

This is the safest way to scope out potential partners and keep a good selection of them at his fingertips, and the Cancer male is all about safety. He's a terrific listener and has all the instincts of a knight in shining armor—at least for the short term. Being a good friend also lets him create and supervise his harem. Not that he'll ever actually sleep with any of them, but emotional affairs run rampant and it's usually from this pack that he selects his new mate.

Cancer Suave

Oh, he's so *smooth*. There's nothing you can say that he doesn't already know. He's a certified expert in anything he wants to be without even trying. He knows what women need out of a boyfriend, and he's up to the challenge of satisfying every sexual fantasy—within reason, of course. He's a skilled lover and any woman should feel lucky to have him in her bed. Even if he's betrayed or hurt her, *he* knows how sorry he is, even though a little part of him concedes that she deserved what she got—and that's what really matters. Right?

The Dirty Little Boy

Everyone thinks that the Cancer male is a normal guy; it's hard for any of them to imagine that he gets a kick out of necking with another guy in the dark corner during a party while no one's looking, or that he's into water sports in bed. He has some incredibly dark and sadistic fantasies, and even if he never carries any of them out, he'll require his lover to be willing to try some things. He's not really into whips or wearing a furry bear costume, but he can figure out a lot to do with both of your naked bodies.

The Easiest Means to the Most Comfortable End

Not lazy so much as self-centered, this man would rather not work or extend himself too far unless work and money have become his hobbies. He's not one to strive for perfection, and even if your relationship and sex life are only so-so, he's not willing to give up his comfort to repair or improve it. He's happy as long as the sex is regular, you don't nag, and he can still spend a few hours a day playing video games.

Deep Throat

No, he's not related to the guy who brought Watergate to light, nor is he into porn, he just enjoys getting head. A lot. It could be the control issue; it might be the self-centeredness, or even the bit of laziness he *does* have. No matter what the root cause of it, there's nothing he likes better than sitting back and letting his little woman get her protein shake.

What He Needs to Learn About Sex

Control isn't always necessary to have a functional and happy life. Relationships will not always be safe, and every once in a while it's beneficial to accept someone's critique rather than blow up into a frenzy of denial and defensiveness. Although he adores most women, they're human beings too and not just objects to be put on pedestals or driven through the mud just because they have curves and a vagina. Some good advice for his life in general would be to get over his obsession with security and to develop a little ambition about realistic pursuits and not just fantasies.

What You Need to Know About
a *Cancer* Woman

June 22–July 22

She's the first woman whose tender touch has kept you in bed long after the ardor has worn off and the candles have burned down. You're surprised by the warmth in her eyes that somehow gentles your demanding hands to light caresses and squeezes. She makes you care for her, and something in the soft weight of her head on your chest brings out an urge to protect and provide. She is not weak. Far from it. But she's so wholesome and good, and she tries so hard and loves so deep that you can't help but despise anyone that would harm her! You touch her and she's far more real than anything you have felt before.

The Moon, Patroness of All Women, Waves, and Psychos

Is it any wonder that modern man would take a symbol of female power and exaggerate the unpredictable and dangerous qualities while forsaking the positive ones? For thousands of years, in many cultures, the moon has been a symbol of femininity, and while emotions were once a source of spiritual strength, they are now mistrusted by our scientific culture. Even psychology (the study of the psyche, or soul), which began with studying emotions, has started reducing emotions to scientific definitions. As the patron of Cancer, the moon bestows on her daughters her mysterious ways along with the weight of modern constrictions.

In Greek mythology, Selene was the goddess of the moon. In the best-known story about her, Selene fell in love with a mortal man and had many children with him. Being mortal, his life would end eventually, and Selene either begged Zeus to grant him eternal slumber, did the deed herself, or her mortal lover decided on it. Either way, her lover was forever sleeping, and how that affected Selene's charge is hard to tell. At times it mirrors her own fears about losing her loved one, and at other times, it shows her selfishness. Artemis, Selene's successor as goddess of the moon, decided to forgo love entirely and remain a maiden for eternity. Many Cancers take the maidenly route, and may eventually wed or be doomed to be old maids, afraid of relationships and their own sexuality.

Her Top Traits Explored

She Loves Home

She loves her family, her friends, her comforter, her dog—anything to do with home. She loves being warm and comfortable in her own place and surrounded by objects that invoke happy memories. She loves being with a man who makes her feel secure and who will take care of her and make all of her realistic fantasies come true. Because her need for security is so high and her desire for home so all-encompassing, she's a woman men marry, not date, and she often gets into serious relationships before she's ready to, leaving her open prey to stalkers and manipulators.

Because this woman really enjoys her home, she's more comfortable with being a stay-at-home mom than most modern women are. She doesn't lack ambition or the desire for job recognition; she would just rather spend her days with family and friends. The ladder-climbing associated with work can be an unwanted anxiety and frustration for her, especially when the competition with her coworkers turns ugly. For this reason, she's unlikely to compete for a lover either. She's not one to rise to the challenge that jealousy presents. Instead, she'll decide that the love affair is too unstable and find something more concrete.

During sex, comfort is key. She prefers everything to look and smell nice, be padded and warm (or cool if it's summer), clean and well taken care of, and she'd love for it to be memorable in some way. The Cancer female has a healthy sex drive—if she feels safe with her lover. She's at her best when marriage is mentioned, and when her partner takes the time to describe to her in detail what he loves about her and all of the ways he's going to make her dreams come true. If she discovered the joy of sex without the guilt usually tacked onto it by culture early in her sexual life, or once a "permanent" relationship is established, she'll be more open to the idea of kinkiness, quickies, toys, and oral sex.

She's Insecure

The Cancer woman is charming, often coming across as self-assured and relaxed, so you might never know that underneath her calm exterior she's trembling with anxiety. Even she may not be aware of her deep-seated insecurity. As her life proceeds and she learns more about herself and the world around her, her anxiety will eventually be replaced by the strength of maturity and confidence—especially if she restricts most of her life to hobbies, friends, and the family she loves, as Cancers often do.

Most of this woman's life is spent in the pursuit of security and comfort. Early in childhood, she defined what she wanted from the world, and throughout her teens and twenties she learned how to get it for herself. Because finding the fastest route to security is a knee-jerk reaction for her, she can land herself in situations that look really good in the short term, but that have devastating consequences for the long term. One of the most common of these situations is getting married before she's mature enough to do so. Unfortunately, with the way our society ignores the permanence of marriage, she might see marriage as little more than practice for a better relationship with someone else down the road.

As many insecure people do, she can talk a big game. In actuality, she needs to feel secure with herself and her partner before anything major is done sexually, or else the act of sex will slowly chip away at her self-esteem and become an avenue to further degradation and disillusionment rather than enjoyment and abandon. She's a feminine woman, with all that "feminine" used to imply. She's strong, dominating, fertile, receptive, and deceivingly submissive, up to a point. She brings all of this to the bedroom and to her relationships, creating a lush and welcoming environment for her mate as long as he creates one for her as well.

She's Brave

This woman can accomplish whatever she wants in life when she learns how to work through fear and pain caused by her deep-rooted sensitivity and not so minor insecurities. Although she isn't afraid to work hard for her dreams, she prefers good company in the labor. Moral support means everything to her, and she blossoms best when surrounded by good friends and family. When her dreams are shared by those she loves, she finds all the work she puts into them very easy. Even if she goes unsupported, she'll find some way to get what she wants, but she has to dig deep and fight tooth and nail to protect her ambitions, especially those that are linked to her self-worth.

When partnered with someone she respects, someone who loves her openly and with great emotional support, she's willing to go through anything and everything in order to make their relationship work. If, however, she's unsatisfied with her partnership, she'll willingly give up financial security in order to find her own way to happiness. This is also where moral support comes in. For if she's found security at home and been taught to find it within herself, she's less likely to shackle herself to an unworthy man than she might be otherwise.

Although she's open to new sexual experiences, she's more comfortable with experimentation when it's presented in a clean, respectful, and wholesome way. It's incredible what she's willing to do if she's convinced that it's the newest fashion, a total secret, and utterly moral despite what her pastor has told her. It's not that she's naïve or gullible; it's just that presentation is so important to women like her and when uncomfortable or outrageous things are presented well they're so much easier to accept.

Sex with a Cancer Female

The Cancer woman, like most women, has a pulsing and persistent sexual desire, but she has been conditioned through her own discomfort and through societal influence to ignore or hide it. From early on, she has learned to fear the impulsive, creative forces behind her sex drive because of the changes they create in her life and because of how vulnerable she feels. When nurtured by a caring partner, her sexual appetite can blossom and serve as a source of inspiration in her relationships and career. However, if she falls into uncaring hands, which so many young Cancer women do, she could turn bitter and defensive and eventually use others to satisfy her own selfish ends without any thought about repercussions or the harm she may cause.

When her sex drive fluctuates, something all women experience to varying degrees but which is extremely evident in moody Cancer women, she can help soften the lulls by learning to enjoy the human contact and closeness that sex brings rather than seeking an orgasm. To satisfy her voracious appetite at the height of her drive, she needs a willing partner who isn't threatened and whose ego isn't hugely bolstered and reliant on her. She isn't kinky. Instead, her sex is filled with love and mutual satisfaction. She's isn't turned on by the vulgarity of ropes or role playing. Instead, she has learned the subtle arts of tantra and muscle control to please herself and her partner. The more confident she is with herself, the greater the satisfaction for both.

The type of sex the Cancer woman has is of great importance to her, just as the type of relationship she enters is of paramount importance to how she lives her life. While she has the drive, she isn't sure how to let it out. She works best with a partner who gently guides her through the initial clumsiness and vulnerability. Even in marriage, usually long after her initial sexual awakening, she fares better with an understanding partner than with a cold, distant, and critical dictator. In a very real sense, she's looking for a mythical consort or teacher. She wants a man who will help her learn about the world and herself, someone who will let her take the reins every so often, as all good mentors do, to see how she does on her own and not humiliate her when she fails.

She's a loyal partner in that she's discreet and considers herself moral. In actuality, many Cancer women have physical and/or emotional extramarital affairs, even though most never let their extracurricular activities affect their primary relationship.

She is an extremely feminine woman who simply loves men, and in a way, the more choices she has with them the more secure she feels.

Preferred Games

The Virgin

Every Cancer woman would love for the people around her to think of her as virtuous. She has a heightened awareness of her reputation and is wary of any public scandal. Her social conditioning makes her think that virgins are better than experienced women, so she instinctively models herself in the most socially acceptable way. Many people would be surprised if they knew the truth of her sexual experiences.

The Martyred Caregiver

She takes care of the sick and needy. Sex becomes an obligation of her relationship and she carries it out with the mechanical suffering of a faithful servant. She represses all of her own needs and seeks an outlet through small passive revenges. While a Cancer woman can stay in this type of relationship indefinitely, she's more than likely looking for a better partner and won't leave her current situation until she finds one.

The Girl Next Door

One moment it seems like you've grown up with this down-to-earth sweetie: she's been there through all of your heartaches, helped you with your calculus homework, and cheered as you started your own band. Then, all of a sudden, you're getting hard-ons just thinking about her, and you wonder why it took you so long to see how beautiful she is. Even in the bedroom, her soft innocence continues. She inspires feelings you've never felt before: protectiveness, fidelity, love. Next thing you know, you're married. It's been her plan all along.

Cinderella

Every Cancer female has a Cinderella complex, and each of her other games fits into this one in some way. Each and every one of them wants to be rescued from something, especially if she hasn't learned how to trust herself. She can convince her lover that he must rescue her from her horrid life, and her subtle way of making men protective of her helps her in this and keeps them loyal long after the relationship should have ended.

The Woman

This is the Cancer female at her most powerful. When she puts all bullshit aside and lets her true, upbeat personality shine through her defenses, she's the embodiment of womanhood: a strong and equal partner, a devoted mother, and a protector of those who are innocent. Her sexuality rejuvenates her, and her partner is surprised by the woman in bed with him. There are no games, no pretenses, no defenses, only love and joy.

What She Needs to Learn About Sex

The Cancer female needs to learn how to handle her sexuality in a way that won't damage her self-esteem. She would also benefit from strengthening her self-love and becoming secure in who she is and not what she provides for people. Taking time to look at long-term goals rather than short-term solutions will make the transition into her late twenties and thirties easier. She also needs to curb her gullibility when dealing with the opposite sex without losing her trust in the basic goodness of people.

Leo

What You Need to Know About
a *Leo* Man

July 23–August 22

The light in his eyes overwhelms the light of the sun when he looks at you, and you feel his warmth seep into your soul. When he loves, there is no doubt that he loves, and even with his bellowing and growling, you feel so grateful that he loves you. He looks for your reaction whenever he touches you, judges it, and explores some more. His genuine concern for your pleasure delights you, and you quake to think about what loving him will be like—how thorough and assured, how delicious and fulfilling—after you have known each other for much longer. But these gentle first caresses are precious, and the light in his eyes will never fade. You have found your knight, dear lady, and in you he has found his idol.

Apollo, Bringer of Light and Melanoma

As all the planets in our system revolve around the sun, so everyone in a room or group revolves around the Leo—at least from the Leo's point of view. Bright, hot, flammable object that he is, the Leo male is absolutely certain of his own self-worth and he burns anyone who tries to tell him differently. His gravitational pull keeps people exactly where he wants them, be it near or far, and if he wants, he can use his force to slingshot them far, far away.

In mythology, Helios, the Greek sun god, was replaced by Apollo, the god of light, around 300 BC. Apollo, one of the most celebrated Greek gods, is well-known for his beauty. One of the most intellectual of the male gods, he stood for reason, logic, oracles (not the joke they are today), virtue, and moderation. Not what one would expect to find as the patron of a Leo. You can find all of these qualities in one, though.

In astrology, the moon and her dieties are considered the celestial mother and the sun is given all the traits of an ultra-masculine father. Apollo (and Leo) stands for repressing, directing, and controlling others—forcing everyone else to live by your rules even though you don't follow them yourself. Both the planet and the god can be supportive, protective, and loving caregivers as well, but never without a major part of control in their hands. He will support you if you do as he thinks best. He will protect you if others get in the way of what he wants for you. The Leo aspires to live out the example set by his patron, and tries to control those around him with just as much omniscient care.

His Top Traits Explored

He's One of a Kind

You'll never find anyone as unique as a Leo male. Each of them is highly individual, and all of them have the tendency of borrowing ideas for their individuality from people they admire. Still, the collection of borrowed "unique" traits, if not the traits themselves, is what makes the Leo a one-of-a-kind person. Whether dressing for school in a Hawaiian grass skirt and coconut bra (yes, I know I'm talking about the *male* Leo here, and yes he *does*) or going to a business meeting in a handmade designer suit, he will make sure to stand out in the crowd.

Leos exert a powerful sexual magnetism over women. Despite the quirks with which he adorns himself, his personality is based in loyalty and passion. At first, he appears to be the perfect partner, making up for whatever skills and imagination he lacks with sheer energy and enthusiasm. He's not necessarily the smartest man, but his innocent and undying belief in his own ego make up for this fact by sheer force of personality. In fact, the Leo in general is one big red herring. Afraid of boring you, he will distract you with the various facets of himself, and if you've only just met him, he'll appear to be a succession of totally different men every five minutes or so. Once you've gotten to know him better, you'll soon realize that there is a definite center to his personality: his ego and that which his ego defends.

He's a Riot

Few men are as entertaining as a Leo. He's energetic and fun-loving, and just wants the world to join in his drama. His is an extraordinary life, lived in an eccentric way, and while he might try to follow a particular path, he often finds himself far from where he thought he'd be. He loves few things more than shocking those around him, especially because his usual antics are formulated to show others that he is above such petty things as social standards and rules. Although he is a loyal partner, he might not consider monogamy to be part of the deal, especially if he's not sexually satisfied with his steady partner.

Besides being the life of the party, there's another reason that Mr. Leo is a riot—he's an instigator, a troublemaker, a rule breaker, and a drama queen. When he's bored, he tampers with the harmony of everything around him and isn't happy until he's stirred up a hornets' nest with which to entertain himself. In his personal relationships, he's more likely to cycle through friends and lovers quickly because of his attachment to havoc. The more evolved Leos realize this tendency early on and present a more tranquil atmosphere and calmer entertainment requirements.

Sexually, he's demanding and willing to try new things, but he's slightly unimaginative and won't know what new things to try until someone else gives him an idea first. He expects admiration in bed—he wants you at your most seductive, the sex at its most explosive, with him as the ultimate star—and when his expectations aren't met, drama abounds. Because he's easily bored, he inflicts such high amounts of drama on his partners that only the most self-assured or masochistic woman can tolerate him for long.

He's Proud

For better or worse, this man is absolutely sure of himself at all times. He is the type of person who takes control of any situation. He either turns it to his own advantage and claims the rewards for himself or he hightails it out of there before anyone realizes he tried to win and failed. He believes that his opinions aren't simply opinions but law. When he sees fit to hand down a decree to us lesser mortals, he expects gratitude and total compliance, and he doesn't respond well to what he considers rejection.

All of this hot air and bullying doesn't mean he needs a woman who'll roll over and take it. He longs for a woman who is worthy of him, and once he finds her, he'll live the rest of his life twisting himself in knots in order to live up to *her*. He wants a woman worthy of adoration, one who knows her mind and who isn't afraid to stand up to him—no matter how loud he yells. He adores being petted and pampered, and he makes one of the most loyal companions around. When he loves, he loves with his entire being, and the light he shines on his partners is brilliant and unique.

Sexually, he hopes he's the best. He can't bear the thought that his partner has been with someone better than him. He needs to eclipse every other person in her life, and he needs constant reassurance that there is no one else. He's very proud of his own sexual prowess, and he's spent some time cultivating his skill. With a partner who praises and compliments him constantly, he'll show such genuine zeal and delight as to leave little doubt about his feelings and exuberance at being in love.

Sex with a Leo Male

Frequent, fast, and flattering. Sex must be made available at any time, and his mate—his queen—is expected to always look and smell her best, and be prepared to receive his attentions with unbridled, quivering expectation whenever he deigns to give them. He isn't looking for a pushover in the sense that he wants a slave. He needs a challenge every once in a while, but he *is* on the lookout for someone who is already his ideal, or who can be molded into his idea of perfection. He is looking for an object to worship, and as all objects of divinity, this one will be based entirely on the devotee's perception.

He won't hesitate to tell others about his partner's most intimate and embarrassing matters—except for the rare instances where his own pride is on the line. Even in that case, he's likely to blab just to make sure that, if it ever comes to light, his story is the first and loudest version everyone hears. Occasionally, you'll find a Leo male who's more mature than the average and this type of Leo is a protective and generous partner who loves unconditionally and freely. He's usually had to fight long and hard for his station in life, and he exalts serenely in his well-earned self-confidence without turning to the excessive pride that his brethren often rely on.

A surprising number of Leo men are either never-been-there virgins or born-again virgins. It's this same idealism that can make him an intolerable lover whose outrageous demands often prove to be greater than the thing his lovers must fight for—him. His idealism leaves him with a rather high number of exes. Sexually, his demands are more for frequency than quality; although, if he's addicted to porn, ordinary sex will never be good enough for him again. He wants more than what everyone else is getting, and he will see that his partner is taken to new sexual extremes in order to ensure he is better than anyone she's been with before.

Preferred Games

Long Live the King

He's the absolute ruler and commander, and he's looking for both queen and milkmaid. He wants to be lord over everything he touches, but he expects his partner to be his equal—or be doomed to being treated like the lowliest subordinate. He enjoys breaking the will of someone, and he lacks respect for anyone he can topple. His life partner will have to be able to stand up to him in such a way that doing so doesn't threaten his pride.

Daddy Dearest

He loves being the protector, the breadwinner, and the confidante. He wants to be the most important person in his lover's life, and he'll reward her with absolute adoration for it. He's not one to enjoy humiliating her in the bedroom, and he won't play any unethical or immoral role-playing games. He values the position he holds in her life too much to pretend otherwise. However, if she's weak he'll have no trouble exploiting that fact in bed—and then he'll break up with her.

The Uptight Virgin

He has beliefs, damn it, and he won't let anyone take them away from him. If he doesn't want to have sex, or if a woman doesn't live up to the image of his ideal mate, then he simply won't have sex with her and he'll resent any attempts she makes at seducing him. He's too proud of everything he is to let himself be pushed around until he's absolutely certain he's found a woman worthy of his affection.

Basking in the Spotlight

He loves attention, especially if it's positive. When he walks into a room, he wants all eyes and conversations to turn to him. He wants to be powerful, respected, and admired. He doesn't grab desperately at the spotlight in the way a Leo woman does, for above all else, he cultivates *style*. Why should he have to fight for attention when it is his right? If a partner comes with her own spotlight, that's fine because he can be proud of that without it having to take anything away from himself.

Pedestal for Rent

Oh, how he wants to find the perfect woman to sell his soul to, and whereever he is, he looks for a woman to worship and adore. Partnership doesn't interest him when he's playing this game. Instead, he wants to be someone's abject slave. He wants a woman who always meets his ideal and never lets him down, and he wants to commit himself to her service for all eternity. Only in that occupation will he be able to truly live up to his possibilities, for serving a goddess is the only worthwhile goal.

What He Needs to Learn About Sex

Following someone else's suggestion doesn't mean the Leo has lost any of his control or power. Knowing when to let someone else handle a situation, and allowing them to take care of it as best they can, and to take credit for it if it works out, is one of the most important qualities in a lover and friend. Building actual confidence rather than creating a fortress of ego and forcing his lover to support that fortress will help him to overcome his insecurities and to appreciate his partner for who she truly is, not just what she can do for him.

What You Need to Know About
a *Leo* Woman

This bright, sizzling woman nearly burns you with her radiance. Her heat is incredible; her eagerness to try new things leaves you tingling in anticipation for all the nights ahead of you. She alternates between submitting or dominating, working just as hard as you are to ensure that both of you reach every position humanly possible, that every nerve ending in both of your bodies is on fire. You struggle to keep up with her, knowing your mutual adventure will end if you let her down and you'll never find her equal again.

Apollo and Shamash, Bringers of Light, Justice, and Melanoma

As the center of our solar system and the most influential planet in astrology, the sun has a rich mythological history. Being mostly a masculine symbol of growth, destruction, wisdom, and aggressive power, the sun gives more drive, passion, and self-importance to Leo-born people than to most other mortals.

In *The Epic of Gilgamesh*, one of the earliest written stories, the sun god Shamash is described as a god of justice. Alternatively, the Hebrew word for the sun, Shemesh, in its verb form means "to be used," as in the form of a caretaker. Leos are often found in a position of caretaker for others. The Leo female often finds herself a defender of a belief or way of life. She is an unemotional but impassioned judge who cares more for what people represent than for people themselves, and she deals mercilessly with those who unjustly harm others.

The Greek deity Apollo wasn't originally a sun god, but he was later merged with Helios and took on Helios's responsibilities. Both Apollo and Shamash are protectors of justice; although, Apollo's actions against Daphne and other unfortunates rob him of Shamash's title of "Defender of Those Hurt Unjustly." For the less-evolved Leos, Apollo is a more fitting benefactor than a god like Shamash. Apollo's selfishness, along with his love of earthly comforts and excesses, mirror the life of a lesser Leo, whereas more evolved Leos wear their worldly goods with careful style and wit. A Leo woman is more likely to help others than to step on them as she makes her way to the top.

Her Top Traits Explored

She's Provocative

Even though she's a woman with uncommonly strong beliefs, she isn't one for much deep thought, and her beliefs tend to be unfounded opinions that support her way of life rather than the true philosophical ideals of some, like an Aries individual. She's loud, obnoxious, and somewhat petty, which usually makes her a catalyst for heated debates and hatreds. She stirs up emotions in those around her and causes drama for the power and attention it gives her. Whether the publicity is about a charity auction she organized or her latest public nudity scandal, she understands that any publicity is good publicity because it gets her name and her product out there. She can turn a sensitive person into a paranoid nutcase and reduce the most uppity, intelligent people to blithering minutiae by her lack of logic and tact, and the absolute assurance that she's right.

She's an instigator and a socialite whose social appearances are dreaded and yet fascinating affairs. Even highly evolved Leos are drama queens, and while Leos in general don't feel their emotions deeply, they can "pretend" themselves into a storm of pitiful heartbreak or fury in an instant. And because her emotions aren't rooted in actuality, she's able to shift them often and without warning, surprising her friends and lovers and creating unstable bonds and feuds with those around her.

As a lover, she's a hell of a ride. Although she may never achieve truly blissful sexual experiences, she's extremely sexually active from a young age, usually because it gives her bragging rights to say that she's desired by many people. She realizes that sex is power and uses it as such, screwing her way to the top of the fiscal or social ladder, and manipulating those around her with absolutely no remorse. If taken too far, this view of sex can validate using her lovers for her own good, and doesn't leave much room for respect, causing a lot of emotional strife and possibly eventually even losing her the love of someone she honestly cares for.

She's Demanding

A Leo woman is always on the go, moving, progressing, and changing. A little uncomfortable with herself, she prefers to be in the company of others, specifically those that admire her. Even when she finally falls into an exhausted stupor, she equates lack of movement with depression and loneliness, not with exhaustion, and she quickly finds some company or distraction. This can lead to promiscuity and a constantly changing group of friends and environment, especially in between serious commitments. She requires constant activity and entertainment, and luckily, she's quite capable of keeping herself busy most of the time. Her idea of entertainment might not match up with her partner's idea of monogamy or sobriety, though.

While committed to a significant other, she's uncomfortable with routine unless it involves pampering her. In fact, she's uncomfortable if an activity doesn't revolve around her. The more immature Leo woman causes an immeasurable amount of drama to ensure she's not forgotten again. Not only must she be the focal point of the universe, all of her relationship provisos and stipulations must be met and preferably exceeded before she'll make a serious commitment. She *must* be showered with affection and adoration, and her partner *must* be willing to continuously prove love for her and tolerate her impulsivity. He must also be a worthy partner, have sexual prowess, and the ability to provide her with whatever her heart desires.

The older and wiser a Leo woman is, the more she directs her demands toward her career and hobbies and away from her loved ones. She's an incredibly talented businesswoman once she learns to protect the things that matter and only exercises her impulsiveness when it won't hurt those who care for her. She's also a much better person once she learns to love herself rather than looking to others to provide love for her.

She's Creative

Perhaps having the sun on her side has given her soul a particular glitter, because the Leo woman sparkles with energy and enthusiasm. While not "original," she is artistic. There's nothing she enjoys better than bringing a spotlight to something beautiful and revealing it to the rest of humanity. She excels in creative pursuits, often turning her hobbies into a profitable—or at least fun—career. And artistic expression is a sort of catharsis to her in times of trouble, which occur more frequently with this overdramatic sign than with most signs.

One of the Leo woman's favorite canvases is herself, and she'll spend ungodly amounts on hair care, wardrobe, and make-up—only to end up pruned, frizzled, and overdone when she reaches her mid-forties. Although she likes to think of herself as an unpredictable and exciting woman, others tend to find her very predictable over time. To understand what crazy thing she will do or what trauma she'll face next, think of her as a walking, talking neon sign advertising Murphy's Law. What it comes down to is that she adores all of the chaos in her life up until the point she finds her once huge body of friends slowly dropping off because they are exhausted.

Sex with a Leo Female

Leo women are dynamic partners who bring a lot of energy, if not skill, to the bedroom. Most Leos are sexually active from a young age, but few of them actually enjoy having sex. Instead, they tend to use it like a drug, thinking it's an easy, quick, flashy, and low-risk high, or a means to confirm the adoration of another, rather than a glorious artistic joining of two people in love. In fact, she must have been in love for her to learn the depth of emotion sex can bring, because love is the only thing that stands a chance of yanking her from her primarily self-centered world. A few Leos enter into the passionate side of sex without making big commitments first, but as a woman's orgasm tends (through social conditioning, biology, or whatever) to first require *abandon*, and a Leo woman can rarely abandon herself, these passionate Leos are few and far between. Those who do manage to achieve passionate abandon are usually confirmed bachelorettes.

For someone who wants a woman who knows how to please herself, and who will be a commanding presence in bed rather than a shrinking submissive one, the Leo woman makes a perfect partner. Her demanding nature translates into a dominant seductress between the sheets; however, her bark is usually more exciting than her bite. When she's not completely in sync with her partner, she's likely to intellectualize sex rather than allow herself to take pleasure in it. She enjoys being enjoyed and looks at sex like a valuable gift to her partner, one that he must appreciate if he wants to sample it again. For this reason, she expects sex whenever and wherever she decides to have it, and is likely to suffer from wounded pride (a mortal wound for the Leo) if she's turned down.

Being a woman who understands that sex is power and who derives much of her own power from it, the Leo woman isn't one to hesitate to use sex to manipulate or wound those around her. She doesn't flinch at stealing another girl's boyfriend, nor does she think twice about announcing your E.D. to anyone in her vicinity, just so they understand that your sexual problems are exactly that—*yours*—and have nothing to do with her.

Preferred Games

The Prima Donna

Center stage, with the spotlight on her, the Leo woman demands attention. She requires adoration and applause and will not tolerate a fan whose gaze wanders. From time to time, every Leo woman loves to play the spoiled brat. She doles out orders to her subordinates, throws tantrums when things don't go her way, or reverts back to the simple imaginative behavior of a child without need to worry about the negative consequences of her actions.

The Puppet Master

The Leo woman falls quite easily and often into an administrative role with her friends and family. She lords over her group with the vigilance of a dictator and the quiet pride of a mother.

As a lover, she enjoys playing leader in both romance and sex and does so with such natural skill that few of her partners realize the heavy pressure of her thumb on their lives. Multitasking and power plays come naturally to her, so naturally that she doesn't realize how they can be misconstrued by those she inevitable steps on.

Sexually, there isn't a damned thing she's unwilling to try. Even if it's dressing up in animal costumes to hump like a couple of moose, she's willing to give it a go. She needs someone to introduce the idea to her, as Leos rarely come up with anything truly original on their own. She has absolutely no inhibitions about sex. She's so in love with her own body and thrilled by her own sexual response that there are a variety of positions and costumes you can get her into without her really ever noticing or caring.

The Actress

No one is as naturally dramatic as a Leo. In her younger years, she wants to do and be everything, from switching accents in the middle of a conversation to trying on fifteen outfits a day. As she ages, she finds her role in life and lessens the petty dramatics. In bed, however, she's willing to try anything and everything, especially those sexual games that let her pretend you're someone else.

Drama Queen

If she's bored, she goes out of her way to cause problems. Whether it's being thrown out of a restaurant for stripping on the table or breaking up a relationship, she doesn't care as long as it's entertaining and doesn't directly affect her. She has trouble relaxing into calm relationships and prefers one with huge emotional ups and downs. She may go so far as to routinely cheat just so she can see a complacent and normally accepting partner explode.

The Billboard for Your Sexual Shortcomings

She isn't afraid to have everyone (including family) know about any problems her partner has between the sheets. Whether it's purposely to humiliate him, exonerate herself, or just coyly "seeking advice" from others, she doesn't care who she tells or who finds out and what any repercussions might be. She, however, would be incredibly pissed if someone let slip any of her faults. Think twice about teaching her a lesson because she'll see it as a sign that a no-holds-barred, knock-down fight is called for.

What She Needs to Learn About Sex

The Leo woman needs to understand that sex requires at least one other person most of the time. She needs to accept that everything is not about her, nor does it need to be. Contrary to her general belief that she ceases to exist the moment the spotlight wanders to someone else, she may in fact benefit from some peaceful moments in reality shared with a loving partner who's just as important as she is.

Virgo

What You Need to Know About a *Virgo* Man

August 23–September 22

Ever so slowly he lowers his mouth to yours, savoring the kiss. He touches your cheek with one hand and caresses your lower back with the other. He feels you quiver and holds you to him. Finally, breaking free of the virginal handling, he takes from you what only moments before he was barely asking for. You accept him, and he rejoices. You see it in his eyes and in the way he smooths back your hair to expose your neck. His lithe body is hard against yours. You feel his teeth on your flesh, and you are ready sooner than you'd ever thought you'd be.

Out of Nothing, Into Nothing?

In modern astrology there is a general conflict about who the rulership of Virgo falls to. Traditionally, Mercury is considered the ruler of this sign; however, Juno, Chiron, and the currently absent Vulcan have also been credited with it. In actuality, rather than studying the aspect of a Virgo and comparing it to those of the planets as one would study the face of an infant to determine its father, the Virgo reflects the debate itself rather than the answer. It won't be until after the maturity of the science that we can determine his patronage. Do not confuse yourself by thinking that I am comparing the Virgo's lack of patronage to the same troubles or benefits of earthly single-parent or adoptive households. Rather, I am comparing his situation to a person who questions the advent of his very birth and not his relationship with his parents.

Without having an astral patron, the Virgo male is often left to grow up on his own. He educates himself with the rigidity of the strictest ruler-wielding schoolmarm. He's often interested in philosophy, psychology, sociology, or the physical sciences. He enjoys precision, theory, equations, and any subject that will allow him to exercise his perfectionism and exactness. But where is his heart? The best education doesn't make up for the lack of warmth growing up. Luckily, many Virgos have earthly parents who shower them with care to balance the effects of being slung into the universe alone. Even with the best care at home, his personal relationships are often void of deep attachment, and as early as his teens, the Virgo male may resign himself to a solitary life and view women either as the means of sexual gratification or as intellectually interesting companions—neither of which boast much of an emotional value.

Being left to his own devices, self-confidence becomes a hard-won victory in his twenties and thirties, but it may still take him many decades before he feels secure in the world. Rather than giving him self-effacing charm, the school of hard knocks and his earned confidence can give him a pompous, critical air, and make it impossible for him to view others with the empathy he rarely received from the universe himself.

His Top Traits Explored

He's Critical

Being sound of mind and possessing a cool rationality and insight into others, the Virgo male is critical about both himself and everything else. Although he's intolerant and slightly jealous of anyone who deviates from his concepts, he has an expectation of society and of specific people, and he's calm enough to accept the *idea* that human beings are imperfect. Without extreme caution—for which he is famous—he could easily slip into disillusionment and emotionally detach himself from the rest of the world in order to protect his hidden but stinging emotions. His studies often serve as justifications for his retreat.

Although he's often fed up with himself, he tends to be involved with people who either think and act the same way he does or who he can control and intimidate. Then he feels bored with his relationships, which further justifies his eventual retreat from intimate partnerships. He's painfully aware of his own shortcomings and those of others, and he can become obsessed with the need to find something perfect in which to put his trust. As a lover, he's open about his doubts regarding the longevity or importance of the relationship, your fitness as a partner, and his own potential benefits from the union. However, his critical nature is more apt to be set aside during sex than at any other time in the relationship. He was born under the sign of the Virgin, yet his physical form is anything but. He may let you know that you need to put more time in at the gym, or that your skin isn't exactly his idea of perfection, but as long as you show some energy in the bedroom, his critical side will be put on hold to enjoy the sex. For a while.

He's Cautious

Repressed, suppressed, and often depressed, the Virgo guy is a tense, sterile (in the disinfectant way), tangled cat-o'-nine-tails. He's a master of hiding and ignoring his emotions. He downplays the importance of loved ones (except for his immediate family, to which he's exceptionally loyal), and he replaces friends and acquaintances easily.

While he's interested in philosophy and understanding the inner workings of others, he seldom places his keen microscope over his own inner self because he's afraid he won't be able to live with what he finds. Luckily, he's apt to discover himself piece by piece, and eventually replace defensive egoism with real self-confidence. This makes him a more likable person overall. Many of the people around him are more likely to see through his veneer than he is himself, and they find themselves reacting to his critical manner rather than to his intentions, which stirs up a lot of enmity against Mr. Virgo, and that drives him further into his defensiveness.

Sexually, he's not as repressed as others may think, even though his emblem is the Virgin. While he finds emotional connections difficult, sex is an area where he can express his feelings. Because he picks his partners well, he doesn't worry about having the vulnerability he displays sexually used against him. Many Virgo males alternate between helpless submission in bed, and aggressive dominance that borders on physical abuse. His anxieties, fears, secret wishes, and (rare) joy are expressed wildly in the bedroom. One moment he will be tenderly making love, and then shortly after the climax he's listing everything that he hates about the relationship as he tries to balance his strong emotions for his partner with the fear of eventual incompatibility. He isn't comfortable with emotional women because he feels too keenly the responsibility of the eventual end, and he'd rather not be held captive in the relationship out of fear for his partner's emotional state. In this sense, he's looking for a partnership of mind and body. Emotions are a possible consequence, but never lusted after or rushed.

He's in Control

You will never find a Virgo who doesn't think he's in full command of himself and his life. He orchestrates his friendships with a greater design in mind and plans out his conversations weeks ahead of time. His recreations are carefully planned, and he's well schooled in the correct application of Marxist idealism. His mind automatically seeks out the flaws in arguments, people, society, and the world, and he doesn't think he's afraid to confront his own downfalls, even though he's shockingly ignorant of them.

His emotional independence is the trait that ensures his control remains solid. Because he's unattached to his friends and lovers, he's free to move around and past them if they become too cumbersome or dependent. He enjoys people who can think and speak for themselves, but he won't tolerate being the subject of their critiques. However, they are often the subject of his. Once emotionally entangled, he's quick to become defensive or depressed if he's unsure of the strength of his lover's feelings for him. He wants security and has learned how to provide it for himself. Adding another person into the equation can feel anywhere from merely uncomfortable to terrifying unless he's in full command of, or completely understands, the other person. In relationships he's likely to either hold back his emotions until the other person eventually drifts away to more fertile pastures, or he finds himself in a situation where his partner is unable to make an emotional connection even if he has.

Sex is one of his means of control. He uses it as a replacement for emotional involvement, and he can downplay his own feelings by equating feelings with sex and not the other aspects of the relationship. While he enjoys pleasuring his partner, he does it to show off his skills, not out of love or tenderness. He doesn't show his control by dominating his partner, but his *separateness* from her leaves little doubt about who's in control of the situation. At this point his partner has one of two choices: she can either submit herself to him or retain some control for herself by imitating his separateness.

Sex with a Virgo Male

The Virgo male suffers from the gnawing belief that there is something inside him that he would rather never find out about. He lives in a defensive state, terrified someone else will discover this flaw and exploit it before he's had a chance to fix it. This belief puts a certain damper on his relationships, which leaves him emotionally disabled until he learns to face his shadow-self without judgment. That's not an easy task for anyone, let alone someone as critical and sensitive as a Virgo. Until he meets his shadow-self, his choices in partners is limited. He must find one who won't threaten his fragile ego by being either too observing or too critical. As many people who are not comfortable with themselves do, the Virgo seeks control in his relationships, and he stores up secrets about his partner in case his own vulnerabilities are ever used against him.

He enjoys experimenting with sex but prefers the experiments to be more in line with changes of positions rather than games or even changes of venue. Each Virgo male has an idea about what the rules of sex are, and all Virgos share a discomfort for crudeness, although they differ on the definition of "crude." They enjoy frequent sex and it doesn't matter if the other aspects of the relationship are boring. Sex needs to be highly interesting if the Virgo is to stick around. But don't go thinking that sex will be the glue that holds together your relationship with a Virgo man. The Virgo is first and foremost a mental creature, and physical needs come in a distant second to exercising his mind.

Preferred Games

Life Coach Extraordinaire

He knows exactly what's going wrong in your life, and he has a few ideas about how to fix it. Once he's found an issue, he can't let it go, and he'll continue to nag and ridicule until you've seen the error of your ways and succumbed to his better judgment. And once you've started making changes, he'll find even more things that need fixing. Before you know it, you're enrolled in logic classes at the local community college and undertaking a grueling exercise routine. He's uninterested in your core personality, and doesn't mind molding you into someone entirely different. In fact, he'd prefer it that way. You wonder why your friends and family are horrified. Eventually, you'll figure it out.

Mr. Ambitious

He knows what he wants out of life, and if you don't fit into his plans he'll drop you as soon as is convenient. If you aren't equally ambitious, or if you can't help him on his road to success, he won't stick around for long, and he may even eventually claim he was never attached to you. He'll use excuses like "drifting apart," or "we're too busy to form an attachment," or "our lives are just going in separate directions right now," to sling you away.

The Struggling and Misunderstood Philosopher/Artist/Poet

Sure you've heard that he's not well-liked, but it's because no one understands his depth the way you do. You see the hurt little boy inside the frozen façade and you won't let him down by abandoning him the way everyone else has. That he is emotional unavailable is your challenge and you won't be put off easily. This is his favorite mask to don, and he enjoys the benefits and esteem it gives.

The Sculptor

Mr. Virgo has a tendency to hook up with unformed, submissive women who are so in awe of his intelligence and ego that they allow him to mold them into whatever shape he desires. While he'll make them into a suitable companion and lover, he'll never actually respect them, and if they develop a mind of their own and start challenging his rule, he'll hunt them down like Frankenstein's monster rather than be overjoyed the way Geppetto was over Pinocchio's transformation.

Tenderness

One of the Virgo's most secret traits is his tenderness. A romantic at heart, he enjoys the subtleties of relationships—knowing each other's favorite smells and places, anticipating needs, intuiting concerns. When he's in love with a woman he respects, there is nothing that he takes for granted. He'll remember every birthday and anniversary, and his favorite part of sex will be the closeness afterwards.

What He Needs to Learn About Sex

The Virgo man needs to learn to trust, to enjoy himself and others for who they are and not what they could be. Acceptance rather than mere tolerance is the basis of human interaction and a cornerstone of relationships, and only when he accepts those around him on an emotional and rational level can he be open for the possibility of love and joy. Intellectualizing is a psychological defense, not a strength, and if he stops seeking perfection in others, he can stop being afraid that they require it of him.

What You Need to Know About
a *Virgo* Woman

August 23–September 22

Her soft, pliant skin glistens with the sheen and moistness of your mutual sweat. Groaning, she arches to you and you drive in deeper, straining, thrusting, grunting with effort and passion. She's always ready for you—her tongue is cool on your jaw, her nails massage your back and hips. Whenever you want her, she's there. Anything you ask her to do, she will try. Just thinking about all of the things the two of you have done brings you to the brink and you spill into her with a final plunge. Yes, oh yes, this woman takes good care of you.

Out of Nothing, Into Nothing?

There is a lot of discussion in the field of astrology as to which planet is the actual ruler of Virgo. Traditionally, Virgo has been attributed to the mysterious and currently undiscovered planet Vulcan, with temporary rulership going to Mercury. However, there's been some debate about the issue with contemporary astrologers assigning Juno or Chiron the responsibilities. Rather than assigning the Virgo to any astral body, I look at her as a conglomerate of characteristics—*the same as with any other astrological sign*—however, the Virgo has an added difficulty of dealing with the question of her rulership and the conflict is reflected in her relationships.

Lacking a universal ruler takes a toll on every Virgo woman from the moment of her birth, even more so than having questionable earthly parents. It can be considered equivalent to being born a God-fearing atheist. Many Virgo women feel unsupported and as a result they compensate in their personalities, which drives them to seek control. They're also oversensitive to the issues around them and afraid of what others think of them. As any person who doesn't believe in a god, and yet who is terrified of any negative reprisals, while secretly pining for a benevolent divine being to reach out a calming hand, the Virgo is very careful to be as perfect as possible. She seeks to find that being within herself and to influence others through it.

The Virgo woman is highly critical, incredibly devoted to her friends and family, self-righteous, purposeful, clean, ambitious, and in pain. She lives less in her mind than her male counterpart does. Although she can appear unemotional, she's quite capable of expressing her feelings, and she can feel quite deeply. Being without an astral protector, she's always in search of a partner who is either a father figure or someone whom she can mother. She is old far before her time, yet strikingly innocent and youthful in certain matters. (Sex isn't one of them.) She is terribly prone to buying into our culture of thinness and what constitutes beauty. She needs a lover who will help her build confidence in her true self and not just praise her for losing three pounds, even if that's something she's thrilled with herself.

Her Top Traits Explored

She's a Caretaker

She's defensive of her lovers. She calculates all of the potential downfalls of a possible pairing, and she's uncommonly willing to deal with whatever's thrown at her once she's made up her mind to commit. Because of her own need to direct the lives around her, she's often aligned with men who are looking for mothers or enablers. While it may seem like a Virgo is the last woman to enable someone, she tends to accept her lover's rationalizations and excuses with little reluctance. Her enabling is part of an unhealthy cycle that many Virgos fall into and few escape. By enabling her partner, she ensures he will always need her to take care of him. In a way, she creates job security. Virgos compulsively grasp at any type of control within their reach, so it shouldn't come as a surprise that she'd use her caretaking as leverage. Once she's matured, she's more able and more willing to reserve her love for worthy partners.

She's also committed to improving her friends and lovers as rational, healthy people (healthy to her may simply mean taking drugs once a month instead of daily, or drinking beer instead of hard liquor, regardless of the quantity). She has an uncanny ability to walk into your life and immediately set out improving you, and she proves she loves you by nagging you to change. She can't bear to see someone persist on a negative path, and once she's made a discovery about a specific weakness or flaw, she isn't reticent about pointing it out. According to her, there are rules to life, and everyone would just be a lot happier if they worked toward bettering everything around them.

Sexually, she sees it as her duty to cater to her partner's every fantasy and whim—within reason, of course. It's part of the security thing. She figures that if she gives him everything his sick little mind can dream up, then he'll be less likely to go looking for it somewhere else, and yes, she buys into the social belief that all men cheat, whether or not their formal partner knows about it. At first, she'll be a sex goddess, and then the control issue starts to show its ugly head. Once she's pretty sure he's not sniffing up another girl's skirt, Ms. Virgo starts to pull back on the fantasy seductress routine. Eventually, five-minute missionary once a month and frequent sessions with his own Rosy Palm are the only sexual encounters her partner is getting.

She's Controlled

The Virgo woman tends to deny any negative or passionate emotion she may have—anything that makes her feel out of control or extremely vulnerable—although, she's able to easily fall in love and she has a tendency even to be a little codependent. She lives by strict guidelines, and her critiques about the outside world are mild in comparison to how she feels about herself. While she feels like she deserves to be loved, she isn't definite about the type of love she could get and often settles for much less than what is healthy. And, because her life is so restricted, she rarely gets to experience the excitement and joy that come with it.

While not independent, the Virgo female is self-possessed and interested in discovering more about herself and the people she loves. Unlike the Virgo male, she isn't afraid of finding some nasty secret deep within herself that proves she is an unworthy person. The female Virgo has passed that particular speed bump and she works hard to correct the problem rather than to ignore it. Her inner control often seeks outward expression through micromanaging and judging others, which can result in her becoming extremely jealous and demeaning toward rivals or anyone who has succeeded in an area where she has restrained herself. She's also apt to form and act out resentments without dealing with the real issues.

She has just as many sexual rules as she has rules for the other parts of her life, but the regulations don't necessarily align with societal norms. For instance, wanting to be a virgin on her wedding night, a Virgo may decide that premarital oral and anal sex are acceptable as her hymen will remain intact, and she'll enter her marriage bed with neither guilt nor shame. She set her mind on this strategy years before and sees no reason to rethink it now. She's not nearly as virginal as some would like to think. She has a vivid imagination, and with the help of a willing partner, she's capable of going to such sexual extremes that anal sex seems timid.

She's a By-product

She's easily influenced by society's and her family's standards, but her lover holds more sway over her than anyone does. She's a constantly shifting conglomerate of everyone else's beliefs and opinions, and she reflects other peoples' expectations. She'll never be truly happy until she develops the ability to stand behind her own ideals.

One of the reasons she's so set on changing everyone else is because she finds herself very difficult to control. Impulsiveness characterizes nearly every major decision in her life, and to make up for her lack of self-control she seeks to restrict herself and others about the smaller things in life. Notice that it's never your beliefs regarding equality or religion that she argues about (unless you bring it up first). Instead, your disagreements are more along the lines of who should clean the bathroom and take the dog out for a walk. She tries not to be a shallow person, but sticking to the obvious is so much easier than delving into the how and why of someone's thought processes. She's capable of the same piercingly honest insight that gives children the reputation of being cruel. Her insight is based on what society has told her to expect and it fluctuates as society fluctuates.

What this means in the bedroom is that she sort of resembles a flexible Barbie doll. She tends to be beautiful (she takes better care of herself than any other sign), she makes sure to have whatever society tells her she should, and she's willing to bend in any position and give herself over completely to a master puppeteer. Of course, any Virgo reading this is screaming right now, but I challenge her to look back into her sordid past and see for herself. True, most of her actions are built around securing security, and sex is just one of many ways to do that.

Sex with a Virgo Female

Well, she isn't usually a virgin for long, although some of the innocence of maidenhood never leaves her. Even her judgments of others are mostly straightforward, shockingly honest, and without ulterior motive. She's easy to understand, if not easy to deal with, and earning her love is a worthy endeavor as she will then do anything and everything for you. Her innocence is translated into rules in the bedroom, and like any young girl who dreams of her first sexual encounter, the Virgo has an idea of exactly how it should be. Unlike the typical young girl who eventually grows out of having so many expectations, the Virgo wears hers like a yoke, lugging the reality of the world as a constant weight behind her.

The Virgo is aware that one of the oldest ways women have controlled men is through sex. As control is a means of gaining security, the Virgo has a definite interest in it, and learns quickly to acquire as many sexual skills as possible to help her keep a firm hold on her man, and she's willing to try anything to keep him happy. It takes some time before she actually enjoys sex herself, and it will only happen when she finally learns to accept herself and her relationship for whatever they really are. She can morph from virgin to dominatrix to Cleopatra to an innocent milkmaid. She doesn't mind being tied with ropes and whipped, and she's more than happy to offer for penetration any orifice physically capable of accommodating a penis—if she's been socialized to accept such things. Each Virgo comes with her own set of rules, and each set is different; however, *any* Virgo in love is capable of being persuaded to do *anything* by the person she loves, regardless of what her initial feelings are.

While she has an air of being unapproachable, she loves being seen as a sex object (few Virgos ever go out of their way to do so, however). She's incredibly earthy and natural, and she'll avoid fancy accoutrements or a lot of makeup to favor of playing up her natural allure. It's rare to meet a Virgo woman who smells bad, is poorly dressed, or doesn't iron her jeans. Sex is just as tidy and perfumed, despite its many variations. And, while sex may drift off during the stable points in your relationship, prodding or a little jealousy gets it right back on track.

Preferred Games

Mother-May-I?

Oh, how she likes being asked! It's a sign of ultimate control, and never doubt for a minute that the Virgo woman demands control. While she may complain about it, she enjoys micromanaging her men and taking care of their needs so that they in turn can take care of hers. She has an opinion about everything and everyone and won't leave her man alone until he's at least tried to see her side of the argument.

Florence Nightingale

Virgos love to take care of people. They adore being needed and clung to and they find a myriad of ways to insinuate themselves into their lovers' lives so that the chance of a breakup is lessened. If a breakup does happen, the Virgo knows how sorely she will be missed. What she hasn't worked out is how to allow her "patients" to get better. Subconsciously, she encourages relapses and addictions because of the security they give to her. She can easily become trapped in a relationship if her partner convinces her he won't be able to survive without her.

Sexbot 3000

She's almost entirely programmable. It makes you wonder why such a malleable woman is so intent on sculpting everyone else. In a relationship, it's pretty easy to tell her what you want, perhaps negotiate a little, and then sit back until she delivers the goods. There are few things she won't do sexually for her man and she can be talked into extremes, including exhibitionism and sex-enhancing drugs. In order to have a healthy relationship, though, she needs a man who won't take advantage of her and who won't let her change her core self, but who will help her find her true self and embrace it.

Social Director

Soon after the relationship begins, she's introduced herself to his friends and family and started making plans for social gatherings. Besides sex, she's found that jealousy is another useful tool for creating permanence, and she wants to make sure that he knows that every male in his circle wants to get down her freshly laundered pants. Even though she will probably never sleep with anyone he's close to, it doesn't hurt to let him think she might.

Seats for Two on the Eternal Journey of Self-reflection

She's an identity thief's dream. She talks nonstop about herself, disclosing everything from her bank account balance to her medical history. She *is* her favorite subject, and she mistakenly believes everyone is as interested in her inner workings as she is. Her self-absorption becomes one of the primary duties of her relationship, and her lover is a sounding board for every thought she has about her life.

What She Needs to Learn About Sex

She needs to learn how to balance her true self with what the people around her are looking for while not forcing them to alter what they want. Learning to live with an independent partner, and finding the security that she needs within herself—again, independently—without having to be in control of her partner will ultimately lighten her load, reduce her stress, and raise her level of happiness. Learning how to enjoy herself sexually and embrace her sexuality will give her enormous strength as well.

Libra

What You Need to Know About
a *Libra* Man

September 23–October 23

Like a gentleman of old, he takes command of the situation while keeping your needs foremost in his mind. He loves your body, and he touches it with an air of reverence that makes you feel beautiful. He's so self-assured and skilled you're afraid to ask how he learned to love so well. Taking you from behind, he works you until you feel the hot flash in your stomach and you expand so far you're no longer contained in your body, beautiful as it is to him, and the freedom is thrilling. He never takes without giving, and he never gives without taking, and, oh, the blessed reciprocity of the world!

Venus, Goddess of Love and Illicit Affairs

Venus showered this man with charm, interesting if not good looks, and a reckless desire to possess as many women as possible. As Venus did, the Libra male is always looking for the next best thing and has difficulty settling into a relationship, despite his sign's propensity for partnerships and marriage. Most of the marriage aspect goes to the Libra female, although even they typically have more than one marriage, as Libra is also the sign of divorce. Venus's interest in extramarital activities is well known, and she wasn't hampered in the least when caught with her toga unwrapped. Known for her beauty, every myth about her centers on her desirability and jealousy.

The Libra man is a jealous man, although not in the usual sense. It's difficult to generalize about when a Libra's jealous streak will come out. Each has his own quirks. Some Libra males will be comfortable with open relationships—that is, up to the point when their partner begins showing a preference for someone else. Others are so possessive they can't stand hearing or seeing their significant other's exes. Rivalry for affection is a typical characteristic of their jealousy. In essence, they won't care what or who you do as long as you're pining for them, but once you leave them behind, even the most emotionally distant Libra man can turn into an obsessive stalker. The degree of the insult to his pride is indicative of how pissy he'll be—and Venus was known to be one vengeful bitch. While her protégé doesn't have the powers of a god, he has a large enough temper for one. He rarely shows it to others, though, for fear of the damage it will cause his reputation. Venus has given him the gift of persuasion and he uses it continually to secure social positions for himself and to maintain control over his circle of friends without having to resort to anything abrasive. Aphrodite's flirtation with Ares, the god of war, is similar to the Libra male's dance with aggression.

His Top Traits Explored

He's Restless

Despite the fact that Libra is the sign of partnerships and marriage, the Libra male isn't comfortable with sexual commitment. He's always on the lookout for something better, bigger, or more convenient, and he doesn't have qualms about cheating. There is always an escape from his relationships, usually planned long in advance and always ready to be utilized in case the need for a quick getaway arises. Much of his reticence about commitment is a result of the difficulties of previous relationships and his dislike for being a slave to his emotions. Many Libra males find their security in controlling themselves and others.

Being an intellectual sign, the Libra male adores discussion and debate almost as much as he adores being right. Rigidity, routine, and closed minds quickly bore him and leave him itching to stir up some drama. He's always aware of the relationships of people around him. There are few people—especially men—who can start a cat fight the way a Libra man can. He doesn't buy into societal standards or others' expectations of what he should do and say, and authority figures have a difficult time convincing him that they're in charge. Relationships can be difficult because he's so untraditional and different from other men that a lot of women simply have no idea how to handle him. On the one hand, he's almost too sensitive and sweet, and on the other, he's cruel and thoughtless. By far his greatest weapon is his emotional coolness and his chilling reduction of people and relationships to simple, sterile rationalizations.

He's sexually innovative and while he lacks the passion of other signs, he makes up for it in attention to detail. He has a lot more tricks up his sleeve than the blindly randy Ares who's just looking for a hole to stick it in, and he has enough stamina to put E.D. pharmaceutical companies out of business. As with many other men who clam up emotionally, the Libra both makes up for and painfully highlights his emotional detachment through really good sex. He isn't one of those men who reserve sex for his formal partner, though, and he can cheat on you five times a day without feeling like his love for you has lessened.

He's Dual-natured

There are definitely two sides to the Libra man. He is both feminine and masculine, light and dark, sweet and cruel. Few Libras can hear a statement without immediately thinking about its opposite. Reconciling both halves of everything is a tedious mental compulsion for them. This can explain, in part, why he feels the need to commit and to cheat at the same time, and why he has difficulty doing one without the other. This is also why it's so difficult for astrologers to pinpoint Libra characteristics, as they exist in dualities. To say he cheats a lot would be denying that he is also extremely loyal.

From birth, he is constantly being pulled in two directions and self-control is difficult to acquire when he's unsure which way to go, and when his opinions change about the how, why, and when of the decision. He needs a partner who's confident and sure of herself so that she might guide him when he's lost, and so that she won't be too hurt when he makes mistakes. And even though he is filled with contradictions, there are a few core personality traits, such as intellect, rationality, and communication, that he can use to progress and grow past the impulse to cheat—when he's ready to.

His mind is so open to new possibilities there is little he's not willing to do sexually. He intuitively knows how to touch a woman and how to bring her and himself the greatest pleasure. He's also a phenomenal teacher in the sexual arts, and his ego is never a part of the act itself so he and his partners are free to explore and experiment. Although his masculinity isn't overt in other parts of his life and it is not his dominant sexual trait, it tends to seep out in the bedroom.

He's a Loner

Heartbreakingly, devastatingly alone no matter who he's with, it's no surprise that the Libra male craves partnership and yet tests it every step of the way. Although he's not an easy person to be with, he's easy to love. He's never satisfied and always afraid that he's missing out on some big opportunity somewhere else. He's seen true love go wrong over something petty in all those movies, and he's terrified of making a mistake and ending up alone. Some astrologers would say he's independent, but in the context of relationships, that independence means aloneness, and no Libra is comfortable being alone.

This hard exterior may make the Libra male seem like the stereotypical bad boy with the heart of gold—an irresistible challenge for many women—and he may have that heart of gold, but he may be rotten through and through, too. It takes a special kind of woman to be in a relationship with a Libra male, as his fidelity is never as straightforward as it seems to be. He has fears (who doesn't?). But should insecurity give him license to do whatever he feels like? It's up to you to decide if it does, and how to handle it when it does. Of course he's testing you, but that's still not a good excuse. Having a steady stream of available partners is one way the Libra male can be assured that he will never be alone. Knowing that his exes miss him and making sure they keep missing him until he's emotionally ready to leave them behind is another reassurance. It's not nice, but it's easy and it's safe and it's two of the many hurdles his partners are faced with.

He's one of the few men in our culture who enjoy cuddling and romance. He's good to your body and when he's in the right frame of mind, he's good to your heart. In the beginning, sex is a wild array of colors, textures, and games. Control and dominance are two usual factors, as is exhibitionism. He enjoys testing your commitment and flaunting your relationship and his control of it in front of others. Eventually, the sex calms down and as routine intrudes, so does tenderness and affection. He'll also drop the control game, and instead of brandishing his power for everyone to see, the relationship is faced with little more than the typical relationship power struggles, like whose parents are coming over for Christmas and exactly how the toothpaste tube should be rolled. Boredom is a potential issue his partner shouldn't take for granted, but a little imagination and massage oil help to break up the monotony.

Sex with a Libra Male

He has many ideas about what sex can be like, and he enjoys experimenting with a willing partner. While he may have some reservations, he likes his partners to be completely free of any inhibitions and willing to trust him entirely with their bodies. He can become so intent on the need for his partner to have blind faith in him that he can appear at times to be an actor on a stage with the people around him serving as nothing more than props with which he performs for his audience. Occasionally, his audience will be more of an audience member herself than a tool, but rarely (if ever) will she be a fellow actor in the spotlight. A good percentage of sex for him is impersonal and unemotional. This frame of mind, combined with his habit of keeping willing partners on hand, can lead to infidelity that turns into a careless habit that has no more emotional pull than if he was smoking cigarettes. Ironically, his casual treatment of sex can also help cement his insecurities about commitment because if he can sleep around, so can you and that isn't the most comfortable thought.

He's good with his hands, and he knows how to set the mood with little more than a glance and the power of intent. Although he isn't passionate and prefers sex to be intellectually stimulating, he's deeply sexual. He uses games and devices rather than exploring the senses or expanding emotional ties.

Typically, his first connection with a woman is sexual and only later may it develop into an actual emotional bond. He enjoys women, loves the female body, and wants to see as many of them as possible. He's nervous about his body but enjoys public displays of sex, mostly because it shows him as a sexually desirable man, and he enjoys having others admire the body of the woman he's with.

He feels responsible for the quality of sex. He doesn't hesitate to rid himself of sexually incompatible partners and will fully admit when one has acted like little more than a limp rag. He takes pride in pleasing his partner and educating her sexually. He also believes in a true partnership between individuals and doesn't use sex to humiliate or demean, and he can be extremely discreet unless seriously wounded.

Preferred Games

The Savior of the Broken Ones

Libra males love hurt women. They enjoy using their soft touch to bring a broken woman back from the brink and teaching her how to love again, so she can, in turn, save him from a life of restless wandering. If he can save her, then it proves that he's worth something, that he's good and their love will always be meaningful (even if the relationship doesn't last). He thinks the trust that results from this situation will help keep him in line and finally deter him from looking for someone better.

The Humble Sex God

It's true that women want him, but don't hold that against him. It's not his fault he's so appealing. This game does a couple of things. First, it lets women know he's desired; and second, it shows them how he's still a nice guy despite the copious number of women he's been with. His nonchalance about his appeal is feigned and there's a good chance that while he's stressing numbers, there's a serious lack of quality encounters here. Keep in mind it's a game. Consider what he's getting out of it and how it measures up with your own goals before you decide whether or not to play.

Sexual Equal Opportunist

Any girl is fair game as long as she's up for it. The Libra male isn't concerned about a woman's husband, boyfriend, best friend, daddy, or whoever. He fully expects that if she's old enough to engage in sex, then it's her responsibility to take care of the potential drama. And if trouble comes knocking at his door, he'll just calmly send it back in her direction. Does he get a kick out of sleeping with other men's significant others? A little. However, as maturity comes, the edge is worn down into first jaded amusement and then, finally, an affirmation of the transient nature of love.

The Best Friend

"Benefits" will most likely come either now or later, as it's difficult for any woman to remain a platonic friend of a Libra male for long. He starts out using his charm and wit, next he's holding your hand through some trauma, and then he's slipping a kiss on your cheek and finally on your mouth. There's a good chance he's been interested in you for a while; he's just been slowly working the tension up to the breaking point—a favorite game of both Libra men and women.

The Intellectual

Libra men get their jealousy, possessiveness, and control issues through intellectualizing sex and all of its implications rather than simply enjoying it. He calmly evaluates the costs versus the benefits of sleeping with a woman, the anticipated amount of political response (for or against) from his friends and hers, how many times he expects to screw her, and what he wishes to accomplish in that time frame, be it anal, oral, or ropes and whips.

What He Needs to Learn About Sex

The Libra male needs to learn to enjoy his body without using it as an excuse to flit from one woman to the next. There comes a point where the benefits of having many women starts to be outweighed by the benefits of having one, and he may be surprised by how well monogamy suits him. Also, learning to participate in sex and in relationships without continual power struggles (and realizing that detachment *is* a form of control) would help him feel happier with himself and his lot in life, as would finally letting one or two people into his mind and heart.

What You Need to Know About
a *Libra* Woman

September 23–October 23

Enchanting! She has a way about her that traps the eyes and doesn't allow them to wander to anyone or anything other than her. Naked and round, soft and sensual, she embraces you with warmth and ready anticipation. She allows you to be a man in the bedroom and insists through demurring that you take control, hinting that you may have anything you wish, which in itself is a test. Are your wishes selfish or hurtful? What kind of a man are you, and do you take her needs into consideration? Eagerly, she raises her hands to your chest. You wonder if it is to feel or to push away.

Venus, Goddess of Love and Illicit Affairs

The oldest story of Aphrodite/Venus's birth is that she bubbled forth from the foam leaking from the severed penis of her father Uranus. The castration was the result of an allegorical and painful separation of heaven (Uranus) and earth (Gaia) by Cronus, the father of all Greek gods. For any man who has intimately known a Libra woman, it comes as no surprise that this was her origin and, instead, answers a few lingering questions he's had about her and their relationship—whether it was platonic or not. Because the most perfect of all women sprang forth from pure masculinity, it should come as no surprise that this "little woman" has some inherently masculine features, as well as the belief that she was created either equal or superior to man. Nor should it come as a shock that she is typically cast in the role of the earthly culmination of every man's wet dream.

Aphrodite has given her daughter extraordinary powers, or so the Libra woman would like to believe. What this woman *has* received is a superior attitude and a dislike for public embarrassment, which leaves her with a squeaky-clean reputation that many would like to see muddied almost as soon as they meet her. To Taurus women, Venus gave earthly pleasures and passions, but to Libra women, Venus's ideals and motivations, and her love of the spotlight, were handed down. The Libra woman feels a compulsion to improve those around her that is so strong and subconscious that she herself isn't usually aware that everyone else doesn't have the same attitude. In fact, she tends to believe that progress is the only worthwhile endeavor for any human to undertake and insists that anyone around her progress according to her own designs.

The strength of a Libra's will, her superior attitude, and her generally appealing appearance provide an irresistible challenge for many men who would like nothing more than to conquer such a powerful example of womanhood and thus reinforce their own male superiority. There is always some echo around her, some reminder that in a far distant time she was involved when a great man was stripped of his dearest possession, the one all men are terrified of losing. This memory inspires both independence and pride in a Libra woman, but in the men she meets, it's an urge to destroy her before it destroys them. At the very least, she tends to find men who view her as a symbol, a fashionable accessory, or a means to gain social or business status. It's an astrological irony that Venus, goddess of love, rules two very emotionally detached, rational, and intellectual signs—Taurus and Libra—and that neither a Taurus or Libra woman falls in love lightly or without great forethought.

Her Top Traits Explored

She's Judgmental

Well, the scale *is* her symbol, and scales *are* meant to weigh things, so *of course* a Libra woman is meant to weigh things. Upon first meeting someone, she instantly begins to judge and analyze them. She pays special attention to strengths and weaknesses and catalogs them in her enormous mental Rolodex®. Her bluntness with her findings (yes, of course she's diplomatic and tactful, but she's also a pitiless judge with a temper) can make the people around her uncomfortable, and only people who are confident in themselves can get close to a Libra woman without suffering a lot of damage to their egos, or taking everything she says personally.

An upside to her cool deductions is that she has a knack for finding the mistakes—the failed dreams, the fears, and the lost chances—that people experience, and she gives them courage to follow their heart, as well as sound advice about what to do when things get rough. For this reason, she often looks like the classic example of the good wife who supports her husband. That's a problem with Libras in general. They always look like a classic example of something, be it manners, wit, motherhood, justice, or the best friend. However, looks can be deceiving. Who they are is usually quite different than who they appear to be, and while the assumed labels may at best amuse a Libra woman, those labels never successfully restrain or define her.

Sexually, she's judgmental. She takes pride in bolstering her partner's confidence, though, and will rarely say anything to damage his self-image unless such an insult is well deserved or borne of long-repressed frustration. She compares every sexual encounter to what she's experienced before, either in real life or in novels or movies. Although she's perfectly capable of pleasing herself, she's secretly dying for a skilled partner who can unleash the raging intensity she has trapped inside herself. This, in part, is why so many Libra women are willing to cheat, and why they are hesitant to commit and seem always to leave a trapdoor waiting in case things don't pan out. She does best with casual sex, a confident partner, and a lot of humor to combat her utilitarian manner and turn that matter into affection.

She's Idealistic

Every Libra woman believes that everything and everyone in the world acts a certain way—or should. She's idealistic and unforgiving of those who don't at least try to progress as human beings or who have shown that they are less than honorable in their treatment of others. She doesn't mind flaws or frailties as long as those flaws and frailties aren't imposed on others— namely her—and she has a tendency to hold grudges for a very long time against those who have proved themselves unworthy either of her affection or of some ideal measurement she held them up to. If Libra women don't have enough loved ones and laughter to soften the blow of the real world, they can become bitter as they age and be difficult to be around.

When problems arise in her relationships, she's one woman who has to talk them out before she can move on. In fact, her partner has to be fond of talking if he's to spend any time with her. She's always at her scariest and most dangerous when her mouth is clamped shut and her eyes are narrowed. And while she doesn't expect her men to be perfect in anything they do, she is always watching for a better opportunity to come and sweep her on to a new adventure and new possibilities.

In the bedroom, a man needs to be careful to not step on her sensitive ideals or turn sex into a power struggle. Libra women generally don't respond well to crassness or vulgarity, and anyone who wants to talk dirty would get further by sweetly complementing her in a totally innocent and non-sexual fashion. While some Libra women would be turned on by being called a whore or ordered around, a man needs to do so with more finesse than the average thousand men have put together. Libra women like to be in charge, and none of them appreciates being guilt-tripped or goaded into having sex. Appreciating a Libra female is the key to a happy relationship with her and resentment will become common where appreciation is lacking.

She's Independently Lonely

Painfully aware of how she comes across to others, she feels guilty about her judgmental nature and is extremely sensitive to how others feel about her. She loves coming and going as she pleases, and she enjoys being her own keeper, but sometimes she just wishes that the traditional sex role of the codependent woman would fit her more comfortably so she could take a break and let someone else be responsible for a moment.

Her superior, almost snobbish, air and her emotional detachment from friends and family make it difficult for others to get close to her. While she craves friendships, she worries about how vulnerable they make her and how much time it will take for her to nurture them. After maturing a little, she learns to make time for relationships (in fact, many Libras diligently budget time for the endeavor) and to give people the benefit of the doubt. Then she is a much more pleasant person to be around because she's learned what she needs to make herself happy.

Being stuck in her head and caught up in worries, doubts, philosophizing, or whatever, tends to take a toll on her sex life. She doesn't have an emotional connection with her body and looks at it as a means to an end—and a rebellious one at that. She's more likely to feel love for a companion when the two of them are in deep conversation rather than between the sheets. Sex, too, is a means to an end, be it harmony with her partner, satisfaction of curiosity, assurance that she's desirable, or simply an orgasm.

Sex with a Libra Female

Sex is easy for the Libra woman, even though her high standards won't let her act on most of the offers she receives because she also understands that, in our society, sex can be used as a weapon in more ways than it can give joy. She isn't necessarily picky about her short-term partners as long as they have a brain and are good looking. But actual commitment—crossing the line into a formal tie and not just a bunch of promises—is tricky for her. She always wants a way out, just in case something better comes along. A Libra woman hands out promises easily and thoughtlessly, which often results in multiple, meaningless engagements.

She honestly loves men and adores both their bodies and what she can do to those bodies. And while sex isn't a passionate experience for her, it's intellectually stimulating and empowering. These two aspects can be stretched to the point where she may objectify men and use them for their sex and attention before casually tossing them aside, only to feel guilty about it much later. The real trouble here usually comes from the fact that Libra women are much more excited by dramatic romance than by pure sex. Bringing a potential partner's feelings into the mix creates a tense buildup of promises and possibilities before the initial act, which is then usually followed by an abrupt loss of interest on her part.

With the right partner, she's willing to try new positions, games, and toys, but she must be assured of his commitment, or at least discretion, beforehand. She's generally up for anything as long as she looks good doing it, and she's skilled in the arts of seduction and pleasure. She especially enjoys having control over a man's body and taking him to new heights of frustration and release. Because of her need to maintain respectability, her firm grasp on control, and her tendency to promise more than she plans on delivering, the Libra woman can sometimes suffer from repressed sexual urges. Then sex can become a major point of contention during her relationship. Throw her one of those traditionally-minded men who'll call her a whore for having kissed someone before he came along, or one of those men who believes sex should be available whenever he wants it regardless of what the woman wants, and her sexuality becomes a tangled mess of barbed wire full of booby traps and resentments.

Preferred Games

The Coquette

She'll promise the world with a glance and soft touch and, at first, she'll appear to be the perfect partner. Even if she's committed, she's used to getting attention and loves to string men along until either her control breaks or she gets bored. This is probably the Libra woman's most notorious trait. She doesn't see any harm in what she's doing. She just likes to have fun and feel wanted, but she won't be too happy if the man she's aiming for refuses to play along.

Judge, Jury, and Executioner

It's rare that she'll make this role a public show, but it's always going on in her head. People are expendable in her world, and she'll only keep those few around her who take her for what she is and love her anyway. (In time they'll teach her to do the same.) She can't mentally afford to have it otherwise. She tends to demonize those people whom she dislikes. She convinces herself that it's okay to cut them out of her life, and tries to convince everyone else to do the same. She understands that people make mistakes, but each Libra has a list of mistakes she won't tolerate. It's best to ask for the list up front and right away.

Wanton Sex Goddess

She'll screw a man six ways to Sunday. She knows all the tricks, damn it, and she's good at what she does. She can give head like there's no tomorrow and stay up all night rubbing him raw. He thinks he could definitely spend the rest of his life with this woman. Well, in truth, she comes and she goes. She can turn the charm on and heat a man to his bones, but because she's the ruler of "balance," there will be coolness and frigidity, as well.

The Morally Superior

She may or may not be a virgin but, either way, she has rigid standards for her sexuality. Those standards are tied to her impulse control, which is in turn tied to her self-esteem. A Libra woman needs to be very careful about which rules she sets down for herself, and she needs to follow through with what she decides, or else she becomes even more rigid and unforgiving with others as a response to her own shortcomings.

The Actress

Her opinions are never black and white and living in the gray gets confusing for both herself and others. Instead of taking the time to sort out all of her beliefs along with all of their hypothetical conditions and requirements and explain them to people, she takes on a role with every person she meets. Playing a specific character is much easier than trying to define her gray world to someone else. But while role playing is easier, it's also lonelier, so the Libra woman spends much of her life feeling fake. She's so used to playing many different parts to many different people that she loses sight of what's really her.

What She Needs to Learn About Sex

Sex isn't a way to gain power and it isn't a bargaining tool. Instead of intellectualizing the event, she'd do better concentrating her energy on learning how to enjoy the act. She needs to have sex because she enjoys having sex, and not force herself to partake in it to please someone else. Nor should she keep herself from enjoying it just because she's distracted or angry. Learning how to enjoy sex for what it is and removing it from the political arena will help both her and her relationships.

Scorpio

What You Need to Know About
a *Scorpio* Man

October 24–November 21

Raw is the one word that completely describes sex with him. He isn't finished until both of your bodies are aching and tender, until he's thoroughly proven to both himself and you that you belong to him. That's another reason why "raw" is so applicable here. It's because sex alone brings out the desperation and fear in him. He's vulnerable, and angry for it. When he makes love to you—he's raw. You open up to him as only a woman could, enveloping both him and his anxieties, and soothing them as best you can, not taking anything but the intentions behind his moods to heart, for that is what it is to love a Scorpio.

My Two Daddies: The Underworld and Bloody War

There are two rulers for Scorpio: Pluto (Hades), god of the underworld; and Mars (Ares), god of brutal war. Knowing this, it's easy to see from the surface that the Scorpio has had one messed-up astrological childhood and it's amazing he hasn't grown up to be a serial killer, rapist, collector of body parts, insurance salesman, or children's party clown. What he *has* gleaned from his patrons doesn't make him the most pleasant man in the zodiac, although he has more than enough positive traits to balance out the morbid ones.

Aside from being the ruler of the underworld, Pluto was a miner early in his career as a god and specialized in precious metals. The Scorpio knows a naive gold digger may be fooled by pyrite and insists that everything he finds be scientifically proven to be exactly what it is before he puts any faith in it. He digs through the bullshit, eternally hoping to find some precious grain of truth or meaning to help affirm this world and his place within it. This is fine when he's studying physics or geology, but when it comes to human relationships, things get a little trickier.

While Pluto colors the Scorpio's view of the world and his interests and hobbies, Ares's effect on Scorpio comes into play when relationships and social interactions occur. Ares can instigate war if he's goaded into battle, or prevent war if his blood lust is appeased. The Scorpio handles society the same way. He's always ready for a fight, but if his partner or friend is sufficiently skilled, the Scorpio may just as easily be led away from an argument. The Scorpio's most terrible vengeance, just as with Ares, results from insults to his ego or from a partner's betrayal. The Scorpio male has the most infamous vengeful attitude known in the zodiac.

His Top Traits Explored

He's Intense

The Scorpio male is the most passionate man in the zodiac. His combination of water (emotion) and fire (passion) make him one steamy dude. His biggest focus in life is on himself, the things he's learned, and the feelings he has. He believes that each man is out for himself, and that he needs to live his own life or else be trampled on by others in pursuit of theirs. He usually makes sure to back up his beliefs with scientific evidence, making it difficult for him to change his mind or to accept a different opinion than his own.

The Scorpion's preoccupation with his stinger is mirrored in his everyday life by the need to thrust into every situation and person he encounters (and by the fantastic number of times he masturbates). This doesn't mean he'll technically cheat; it just means that he has a tendency to plow through everything around, to assert his dominance, or at least his presence. When he feels slighted or insulted, this man can jump into a downward spiral, believing that the insult was intended, malicious, and specifically aimed at him. Such an insult, in the Scorpio's book, *requires* vengeance if only to ensure it doesn't happen again. And if the insult comes from the woman he loves, he suddenly doubts their relationship, her fidelity, his masculinity, her feelings for him, their ability to last as a couple, and so on and so on and so on. It won't stop until he's placated, and maybe not even then.

There is something about this man that broadcasts to women that he's going to be a magnificent fuck. Scorpios are generally in good shape. They enjoy the effect they have on women and the jealousy they foster in other men. When he looks at a woman, it's as if he's searching the very depths of her being, seeking out hidden passions and deciding how he can fulfill them. There's desperation in his lovemaking, and an undeniable maleness in his possession of a woman that makes her feel as though they're the last couple in the universe and the fate of mankind rests on his sex, and it feels this intense every time he has intercourse. It may sound thrilling, but even the most nymphomaniacal woman gets tired.

He's Possessive

When a Scorpio is interested in someone, he wants every part of her he can get. Even if it's just a one-night stand, he wants to know that she's entirely focused on him until he's ready to let her go. When in love, his possessiveness becomes more and more intense, especially if the woman he loves is of the independent variety and doesn't give him the continual reassurance he requires. When his jealousy is piqued, he can become very scary, even resorting to stalking, eavesdropping, and spying. He won't rest until he knows her every movement and friendship, and he won't relax until he's familiar with her routine and she never varies from it. Far from helping to keep a woman honest, this behavior is likely to drive her away, which in his mind confirms his suspicions and makes him even more demanding on the next woman. To make matters more annoying, if he finds himself in a stable relationship, he's likely to take his partner for granted, eventually forgetting that she's even there while he's out pursuing his own hobbies or career.

In the Scorpio's mind, the world is full of two kinds of things: those he owns and those he doesn't. Be it ideas, cars, houses, women, friends, or jobs, he either has it or he doesn't, and the things he does own are either his possessions or his captors. His possessions are completely his domain, and his captors had better be more dominant than he is or else he eventually possesses them, too. Sound confusing? Try having a conversation with him on traditional American values or the Chaos Theory. This is a man who gets to the bottom of everything, who questions the way he lives his life and assigns quantitative values to everything.

In bed, he's an all-encompassing lover. Sex with a Scorpio is an experience, not just an act. His desire is insatiable, his focus on his partner is beyond intense, his demands never cease. He's a lover who can bring out the best in his partners and exhaust them completely. A woman will never sleep as soundly as she will after a thorough banging from a Scorpio male, nor will she be as physically and mentally relaxed—until he's ready to go again.

He's Interesting

Perhaps one of the reasons this man is so intriguing is that it's impossible to know exactly what he's thinking or feeling. He learned very early on that some of his most natural tendencies—like jealousy and calculation—are considered "bad" by the rest of the world and that he had better hide his innermost feelings lest they get him in trouble or are used against him. He offers a sharp relief in fluorescent light for the rest of us who manipulate and experiment with people in a more subdued and subconscious manner. He won't hide behind denial like the rest of us do.

All women within fifty feet of him can feel the steam rising from his broad shoulders and intuitively feel the danger, self-destruction, and eternal loneliness radiating off him. He's both an irresistible bad boy and an affable prankster who hopes to find the right woman to commit his heart and soul to. When his attention is focused, it's all-encompassing and demanding. He might turn to humiliating public displays of his sexuality. (I know a couple of brilliant Scorpios who enjoy public sodomy with random objects.) A Scorpio male's public displays ensure attention and allow him to work off some of his own sexual frustration or work through any victimization he experienced in the past.

Not only does the Scorpio male condition his body, he sharpens his mind and broadens his knowledge. He wants to be a brilliant conversationalist who never puts his foot in his mouth, and he wants respect and not a little fear from his colleagues and friends. He has many hobbies and interests and he somehow makes sure to find time for everything that is important to him.

As a lover, he has many ideas about how the act can be done and he enjoys experimenting, although he usually ends up struggling to please his partner—more so because of his habit of picking voyeuristic women than due to any lack of skill on his part.

Sex with a Scorpio Male

It's difficult to know where to begin as the Scorpio seeps into every aspect of his lover and her life. His interest is intense and controlled, he gives the impression of a man who knows he's going somewhere in life, yet he's thoroughly unsure of his direction. His insecurity can give him a subtle disarming quality, and he ultimately finds his best partnerships with nurturing women.

His is one of the most sexual signs in the zodiac. Much of his creativity and ambition are aggressive and thrusting in nature. He needs to insert himself into everything in order to feel truly a part of anything, like the scorpion with its stinger. He needs to feel that he is inside of a woman to feel like he is a part of sex and of the relationship. Despite his isolation, he's uncomfortable with himself and looks to others to provide a reflection of his value as a man. He's constantly aware of any possible insults and degradations. He envelops his lovers, lays claim to all of their senses and activities, and drives out any thought of anything outside of himself. He too looks to lose himself in sex. He uses the act as the ultimate assertion of his manhood and one of the few times where he can let go of his fears, which is why things get sticky when infidelity enters the picture. A Scorpio sees being cheated on, or sexual abandonment, as the ultimate insult—it's one of his greatest fears.

Because of his need to saturate his lovers, he's willing to try anything they might be interested in or find enjoyable. He's an automatic expert in anything he tries sexually, and his imagination is at its best when confronted with issues of life and death, and *la petite mort* is inherently a little of both. He *studies* people. He can flatter and offend with his observations of the differences between one person and the next. One moment he may act embarrassed and admit to a woman she is the first to hold him back, and the next minute he can proclaim her pores are much too large and her breasts too small. He can offend even the sweetest in-laws with his cold discussion of his lover's—their precious princess—many faults, including her ineptitude at giving good head. It's always better for a woman to develop a thick skin early on, learn to ignore the Scorpio's mood swings, and reassure him about his insecurities. She must also know how to draw clear boundaries and fight without compromising either of their egos.

Preferred Games

The Wounded Child

The Scorpio didn't experience a perfect childhood and he's been trying to escape the injustice of it ever since leaving his parents' home. He uses this alternately as an excuse for his poor treatment of others and as a reason for his continued neuroses. He wants a woman who will take care of him and make up for the protection and love he lacked as a child. He wants to be coddled and babied, cuddled and petted, and to have all of his faults and mistakes forgiven and forgotten.

The Stalker

When threatened, the Scorpio finds it difficult to let go of anything, especially a lover with whom he has an emotional and sexual attachment. He will react with a knee-jerk obsession, where all other concerns are wiped from his mind and his focus in entirely on *her*. He may intellectually understand that what he's doing is wrong—personally and lawfully—but he can't seem to stop himself. He doesn't know how to back off. He calls your cell every other minute, watches your house, monitors your visitors and trips, and shows up on your doorstep until a higher authority tells him to leave you alone.

A Lover Fit for a Romance Novel

He's got it all: he's intense, self-consumed, nervous of attachment, exciting, attractive, and really good at sex. He's a challenge. He's quite a prize for someone who's strong enough to face his personality shifts and accusations and to keep from being drowned in his ardor. He takes care of himself physically, and his smoldering gaze and intriguing should-I-or-shouldn't-I hesitancy makes him worthy of the romance aisle at the bookstore. He's pretty stable long term if he stays interested and his jealousy isn't provoked too often.

Idol Worshiper

He already has the pedestal. Now, all he needs is the woman to place upon it, and all she needs to apply is a vagina. He can be so desperate for love that he is willing to accept the faultiest women and the unhealthiest relationships in order to lessen his loneliness. He succeeds only in increasing his disillusionment about love, though. His insecurities, sensitivities, and multiple defenses make it difficult for him to find the right woman to settle down with. Eventually, his belief that there is such a partner out there for him is worn down.

Self-destructive

The Scorpio spends half of his life destroying everything around him, himself included, through indulgence in alcohol, drugs, or sex. The other half of his life he spends trying to make up for everything he's done wrong. In fact, his life is spent in extremes, going from abuse to repentance to abuse again. He's always trying, in one way or another, to escape himself at every turn.

What He Needs to Learn About Sex

He would improve his life drastically if he reconciled himself with his own nature, accepted it for what it is, and reduced the difference between his ideal self and his actual self *whenever possible*. Even with his belief in God, there are parts of the Serenity Prayer that he needs to memorize. Directing his insecurities outward to others, like his significant other, won't help either the Scorpio or his partner. He needs to take accountability for his feelings, learn to change or live with them, and allow himself to grow as a person.

What You Need to Know About
a *Scorpio* Woman

October 24–November 21

If this is drowning, you don't mind in the least. She seeps into your very pores, broadening and enhancing you from the inside out until there is nothing but her. She's intense. The steady warning look implies that she loves you—for better or worse—and you had better be on your best behavior. But you see vulnerability in her eyes, too. It's that and not her subtle warnings that cleave your heart in two at the thought of destroying her trust. When she comes at you, it's with the blind focus of a bird of prey as she tears your clothes in violent disregard. At other times, she's so gentle and fragile that you ache with the control needed to please her. Sometimes she comes not at all, and that is when you're needed most.

Pluto and Mars: The Underworld and Bloody War

Is it any wonder that with such heavily masculine backers, the Scorpio woman is an aggressive, powerful woman with an insatiable desire to thrust into anything and everything? She's as intense and mysterious as her patrons, Pluto and Mars, and she tends to have nearly as powerful an effect on those around her as they did. While she doesn't kill or start wars, on the large scale anyway, she prefers to govern her life and her acquaintances with an iron fist, and she has more than a little taste for drama. She enjoys stripping people and situations of their masks, unveiling the true core that few others are capable of discerning, and watching the ensuing panic as people scramble to regain social balance and salvage their dignity. She manipulates her circle of acquaintances by knowing each intimately and storing weaknesses and painful secrets in case she needs to use them. She deals with her few actual friends with more discretion and loyalty. Even if greatly wounded or betrayed, a Scorpio rarely stings her friends.

The Scorpio woman is interested in the how's and why's of society, and her inability to buy into a social or religious practice simply for the sake of following the masses can make her life uncomfortable at times, as she can't do something without knowing the reason behind it. Her two rulers walk different paths than the rest of the gods, and yet each performs a vital function for mankind: war instigates change and innovation, and death is the necessary end of all of us. So, too, the Scorpio's deviance from tradition serves a purpose for society. Without deviance, society would never grow or progress, and without some idea of what "shouldn't be," it would be hard to define what's "normal."

She tends to be surrounded by death and discord, although little of it is her own making. She has an accidental occupation of helping people through major changes, including preparing them to accept their own death or that of a loved one. Few of her friends exit a relationship with her the same as when they entered into it. Once the Scorpio becomes accustomed to her usual role in someone's life, she may find it difficult to commit to a relationship for the long term, simply because she has no idea how to still be with someone after they've learned what she believes she has come into their lives to teach them.

Her Top Traits Explored

She's Magnetic

Not only does she exude a powerful ability to attract people to her, she can also repel them with enough force to knock out steel-reinforced walls. Her intensity and sexuality can be projected into a crowd, stimulating admiring glances from fifty paces away. She's one of the few women who can deliver what she promises—as long as she remains interested. A Scorpio woman rarely plays the role of the innocent woman who must be coerced into bed. She's more often seen playing the abrupt and assertive woman who knows what she wants and doesn't let social propriety stand in her way. Such actions would leave other women open to degradation, but few people are willing to reprimand a Scorpio woman because her vindictiveness is legendary.

Just as she can attract admirers, she can also chill everyone around her. Few people can protect themselves from her chill unless they're already well-insulated with thick skins and stable egos. Her ability to see into people gives her a ready weapon to use against them, and not many people are willing to brave her arsenal simply for the sake of getting to know her better, regardless of her sexual voracity and loyalty. She lets everyone know, either through a frank statement or simple action, that she's in complete control of her relationships and the people in them. In fact, one of her biggest fears is feeling out of control. That's why she compiles information, sifts through the niceties to the hard, cold truths of the world, and maneuvers everyone around her. She wants to feel secure with how much of her she gives to them.

Because a woman's sexual role can be seen as the essence of submission—being thrust in to by a man when she has little in the way of natural tools to thrust back into him—the Scorpio is painfully aware of her vulnerability during sex and tries throughout her life to switch the roles. She knows that men sometimes use women for sex, so she decides to use men for sex. She knows that she's being thrust into, so she finds a way to manipulate her partners around *her*. She understands the magnetic pull she has on men, and she can and will use it to her advantage, even if "her advantage" means nothing more than securing a commitment and feeling safe in the relationship.

She's Aggressive

Aggressive, dominant, power hungry, ambitious, and calculating, this woman knows what she wants and is more successful than most at getting it, which also gives her firsthand knowledge as to why one should be careful what they wish for. Whenever her forward movement is blocked, everything in her psyche is blocked as well, including her sexual expression. Actually, this is the essence of her reputation of running hot and cold: the Scorpio is either in full assertion of her energy, or in total lack of it. A Scorpio woman can only embrace her sexuality when all other aspects of her life are progressing, when she feels secure with herself and in control of where she is heading. When repressed, her sexuality will turn into a seething, foaming, torrid fantasy life, the likes of which are so vivid that she may even leave her well-established partnership in exchange for a chance to rut with her fantasy lover for fifteen minutes.

She has difficulty achieving honest relationships, as her penchant for cold calculation makes her feel both subhuman and superhuman, but never on the same level as everyone else. She cannot help but see others as a means to an end, and even though she feels guilty about it, she has little difficulty dropping someone as soon as they have outlived their usefulness. While this may seem cruel on some level, she can also make a startlingly loyal friend, usually to one or two people who see through her callousness and who do not judge her (thereby tending to avoid her judgment of them). The Scorpio is eternally aware of how others may objectify her just as easily as she does them, and she seeks in turn to objectify herself and to assert her subjectivity.

If a man is looking for a typical woman with whom to share his bed, he had better look somewhere else, as a Scorpio woman is more prone to fuck her man than to be fucked by him. She has little problem ridiculing a partner who has not pleased her sexually and doesn't think twice about humiliating him in public. She has an extreme sex drive, an inherent need to thrust, and often lacks the opportunity to fully explore it.

She's Passionate

It's all or nothing with this creature. Her emotions and regard can slide from one end of the spectrum to the other in a moment. Much of her time is spent in regulating her relationships and deciding how those around her feel about her—whether or not they've slighted her or if they've proven themselves to be true friends, and how to handle any problems quickly and permanently. One of the Scorpio woman's most famous traits is her instantaneous attack when threatened in any way, real or imagined. Each of her many vulnerabilities is heavily guarded and defended with absolute ruthlessness. Scorpio women believe that any trespassers are begging for a bitch slap, and they hand them out accordingly and with glee. The combination of water and fire rulership gives the Scorpio a steamy personality that is all emotion and fiery passion on one side, and all fog and saturation on the other.

When in love or even what she considers "mild infatuation," the Scorpio woman demands constant attention and total fidelity from her lovers. Not so surprisingly, this woman has little difficulty keeping a man's attention or of getting his ready agreement to each of her demands. This is due, in part, to her ability to pick men who will put up with her and because she makes an intriguing partner—sexual and otherwise. She's unpredictable and exciting, with a sex drive that just won't quit and an imagination large enough to outrun *Penthouse* and the *Kama Sutra* combined. She often has greater stamina than her partners, and she desires a "manly" man who knows his way around a woman's body. While she might allow herself to bed a moral prude, this will result in extreme sexual repression and ultimately a fantastically passionate end to the entire affair.

Sex with a Scorpio Female

A Scorpio woman at the peak of her sexuality can feel the blood coursing through her veins and life pulling at her to join in the fun. She's energetic, upbeat, vibrant, and she fantasizes about sex with every person which whom she comes into contact. She daydreams about lurid encounters in bathrooms and dark corners. She has great difficulty being faithful to her partner if her sexual expression in the real world has been repressed for any length of time.

The beginning of a relationship or affair is usually when her sexuality is at its most remarkable, but it tends to dwindle away as the relationship stabilizes and loses its newness. For such a sexual woman, she remains shockingly naive about having sex for her own pleasure rather than strictly as a tool to entrance partners. If there is trouble at home, she will look somewhere new for a cure.

The Scorpio female's sexual escapades always include power in one form or another. She seeks to gain control for herself by first seducing her partner and entrapping him with her superior sexual skills. Later, she holds on to his ego and manipulates him, either through the promise of sexual activities or by linking his own power to his ability or inability to please her sexually. The Scorpio fantasizes about meeting a man who is her sexual equal or dominant, someone whose own skills and standards are so high as to finally allow the Scorpio to give up some of her control and enjoy being a desirable woman. Ironically, though, she finds lovers who can be directed without much resistance, are good-humored (to balance her foul moods) and thick-skinned (so they know better than to take her criticisms to heart). Easily bored, she has a tendency to blame her partner for not making things more interesting and not anticipating her every need. The grass is always greener on the other side of the fence for a Scorpio woman, whose imagination rules her very being, which is one reason why it is so easy for her to attract what she wants.

Because the Scorpio marches to a different beat than the rest of us, she's willing to do a great number of exotic and naughty things between the sheets. She understands that sex is about sensations, and she exploits this by seeking out and controlling those sensations felt by herself and her lover. She's a skilled partner, virile and willing when she's in the mood, frigid when she's not full of high expectations and standards that inevitably fall short and leave her jaded.

Preferred Games

The Seductress

She has smoldering eyes, a low-pitched and sweet voice, and she can usually put her legs behind her head. She knows how to appeal to a man on whatever level she chooses and manages to maintain her dignity even when offering the most carnal of pleasures. This is usually her first act in a romance, the foundation on which she'll build the rest, and the initial test of compatibility—one that most of the men she's with fail. It's difficult for her to remain faithful to her partner, especially if he isn't her sexual ideal. Her mind, at least, will always wander.

The Puppet Master

She must have control over her man and their relationship if she is to allow herself to become vulnerable enough to love. She picks men in the same way she picks stocks—looking for potential for future growth rather than established companies with good records. She enjoys helping her partner realize his potential, and she secretly doubts her own ability to secure a man who's already successful, especially if he owes his success, in part, to another woman. She hopes that being a part of his success will instill loyalty and security, and he *will* succeed or else she will find a new project.

The Good Girl

It is a difficult thing for most people to reject society's opinions, and the Scorpio is a compulsive individualist. In order to make up for her guilty feelings and methods (after all, a woman being manipulative, calculating, or aggressive is rarely seen as positive in our culture), she will project an image of innocence and simplicity, hiding her mind and her passions from the world. To the people around her, everything in this chapter may be seen as an incorrect description of their sweet girl. To the Scorpio, however, this chapter may become an uncomfortable unmasking.

The Scientist

A constant observer, the Scorpio experiments on her friends and lovers in a slightly more honest way than the rest of us do. She intuitively practices behavior modification and enjoys seeing the results. She brings this calculation to the bedroom, systematically trying on attitudes and twisting herself into new positions and roles. She cannot stand a boring or inhibited lover and anyone sleeping with her will have to get used to the professional sterility and detachment with which she makes love.

The Bridge

With corulers like Pluto and Ares, it's easy to see how the Scorpio becomes a bridge for people, taking them from one stage of life to another, even helping them deal with death. She has trouble committing for a long period, because she's so used to helping people past a milestone and then leaving them to carry on with the rest of their lives. She herself goes through many metamorphoses in her life, living under completely different circumstances every five years or so, making the difficulty of lasting commitment that much tougher.

What She Needs to Learn About Sex

She has powerful sexual energy but it doesn't need to be an embarrassment or a burden; neither must she live up to others' definitions of what she should be. Learning to embrace herself, rewarding herself for goals accomplished, and being gentle with herself instead of impatient or belittling will go a long way towards her happiness with others and with sex.

Sagittarius

What You Need to Know About
a *Sagittarius* Man

November 22–December 21

His head dips slowly, enjoying the moment when your breath catches in your throat and you moan his name. He pets and caresses, savoring the feel of skin on skin and the excitement in restraining his own urgency. You've tantalized him, teased him since he first laid eyes on you, and now, finally, he will accept his reward for his patience. He feels the intensity become a tangible vibration in the room, and you're ready for him. He thrusts eagerly inside you, slow and reverent no more. He's demanding and caught up in the sensations. He forgets that you and he are two separate beings. He feels only the thrill, the nearly unbearable hotness of you surrounding him. His body thrusts to the rhythm of lovers, one of the oldest human actions and most ingrained instincts, and in it he loses himself.

The Privileged Son of the God of All Gods

We've all heard about how wealthy kids act—they're impulsive, self-centered, hedonistic, and yet manage to stay out of trouble one way or another. Yes, they are said to be royal pains in the ass. Now, imagine how bad they'd be if their parents ruled the universe and not just some earthly Fortune 500 company. Thankfully, Jupiter is a jovial (congratulations to all who get that) persona, and he has handed his good nature and laid-back attitude to his favored pupil, the Sagittarius male. He's also given this man the desire and ability to try out as many pretty women as possible and somehow escape most of the consequences.

The extent to which Jupiter (Zeus in Greece) would go to slip into the bed of a pretty woman is legendary. He transformed into animals and women (yes, lesbian action was not unheard of for the gods), while lies, rape, and general seduction were all employed to win time with the ladies. The Sagittarius is less likely than his patron to be led to such immoral means. Although he's no less inspired by the prospect of sex, it is much less important to him than it was to Jupiter. For the Sagittarius male, there are simply too many adventures and possibilities to get caught up in one chase, and he hopes to enjoy as much of life as possible while he's still able to. Chasing a good time is so natural to Mr. Sag that it should come as no surprise that centaurs, the symbol of Sagittarians, were created by Jupiter when he chased Venus, the goddess of love, and could not catch her. During the chase, Jupiter was so excited that he dropped his "seed" on the ground and from it sprang the half-horse, half-man creatures that now represent the Sagittarius.

The list of Jupiter's lovers is long and reads like a who's who of the top beauties and goddesses of the day. Likewise, the Sagittarius male is attracted to beautiful women, and he frequently gets their affections no matter how far out of reach they may be considered by others. It is safe to say that the Sagittarius male doesn't owe his successful sex life to only his own good looks. His charm and adventurous personality work wonders when it comes to attracting women.

His Top Traits Explored

He's Adventurous

The Sagittarius is a firm believer in self-entertainment. He has infinite ways with which to entertain himself and others and, consequently, he is rarely bored or repressed. He enjoys movement of all kinds, especially to foreign places; and conversation with stimulating people exchanging new ideas and discussing personal experiences can keep him fascinated for days. Don't let this rare show of social interest fool you, though. The Sagittarius is quiet by nature and solitary in the way that every traveler is solitary. He has a unique collection of experiences, a well-developed sense of confidence, and he's open-minded about the world. Although he rarely feels a true *need* for someone else's companionship and even more rarely does he seek it, his calm acceptance of others make him a valuable friend.

Because he's friendly doesn't mean there isn't some danger in associating with Sagittarius men. They have their dark moods, their tempers, their ultimatums and demands. They are often too honest for comfort, and they stumble through adolescent infatuation, making mistake after mistake and crushing many hopes along the way. It is not until much later that they learn to use tact, and even then they are apt to wound sensitive people and startle a lover with a shocking truth during an argument. To a Sagittarius man, there is simply too much going on in the world to worry about someone's hurt feelings and tripping on traditions and customs. He enjoys people. He's honest about his attraction to other women and his desire for experimentation and variety. He is best suited for a lover with as much confidence as he has and little chance to feel jealous or to mind much if he strays. He uses a rational approach to the problem of fidelity, and his reasoning often looks something like this: his mind needs stimulation, so he converses; his heart needs affection, so he loves; his body needs sustenance, so he eats; and when his libido needs exercise, he screws. It should be just as simple that. It doesn't help that women find him so appealing and that his sexual artistry is both fun and skilled enough to ensure many partners, and to make sure he's missed when he leaves.

He's Philosophical

Every Sagittarius has a belief about why the world is the way it is. Once asked to share their thoughts, Sagittarians can startle their listener with how deep and far-reaching their minds are, especially for someone as carefree and adventurous as they are. Much in the world disturbs them, but rather than being taken over by pessimism, Mr. Sag chooses to embody the traits he wants to see in others and lead by example. For this reason Sagittarians are often pushed by those close to them to embrace a life of public service, but their need for freedom keeps them from any such activity, and they will instead perform their humanitarian efforts in a low-key fashion, avoiding praise as much as criticism.

Rather than being an active seeker of knowledge, the Sagittarius male is the kind of person someone would be if they made efforts to be a good listener, travel, and cultivate an open mind. Not to say Mr. Sag doesn't *seek* learning. In fact, he is learning continuously; it's just that he hates making anything formal. Sagittarius is the sign of the potential mentor, and this man could equal the likes of Obi-Wan Kenobi, the Ghost of Christmas Past, and Mrs. Potts (yes, the teakettle) if only he was willing to take some responsibility in another's actions.

Sexually, his penchant for philosophy plays out in his carefree attitude toward sex and in the type of partners he picks. While he himself is intellectual, he's fine with less intelligent partners (his sex can be as mindless as a caveman's). He can rationalize in the morning for or against monogamy, depending on his mood, and he can be arguing for the opposite by lunch. A lover of humanity, he finds difficulty working outside his own box and he can be quite selfish inside and outside of the bedroom.

He's Absent

Physically, mentally, and emotionally, this guy tends to take out-of-body or in-body vacations on a continual basis. Ninety percent of the time, when his body's beside you, he's thinking about the

Caribbean, the girl next door, or the last book he read. For this reason, it's hard to achieve intimacy with a Sagittarius. He leaves women frustrated with his lack of response or enthusiasm to her conversation, issues, or sex. He usually becomes a master of charm with age and he capitalizes on his quirkiness in order to get around upsetting too many people with his absences. While he gets better at hiding them, his absences never cease or even slow down. That's why he does best with a partner who has her own life and who isn't hurt when his brain skips town for a couple of months, or when he's busy having an affair—either emotional or otherwise. The surest way to turn his absence into a permanent relocation is to cling to him and ask him to assuage your every insecurity and doubt.

Emotionally, this man is more absent than most, and he dislikes being in emotional situations or hanging out with emotional people as they demand attention that he isn't usually willing to give. Intellectualism is his escape, and he distances himself from everything around him despite his eternal need to experience all life has to offer. He rationalizes to a harsh degree to minimize the feelings of his lovers and friends and to downgrade the seriousness of the relationship to something easier for him to handle—

something that won't threaten his precious freedom. Surprisingly, despite his emotional unavailability to most women, he can get obsessively caught up in the chase of someone who's hard to catch and all the more desirable for it. Once caught, though, he's as likely to leave her as he is anyone else.

Sex with a Sagittarius Male

Well, you probably weren't the first woman in bed with him, and you probably won't be the last. And while you might expect someone who's as experienced as he is to be extremely skilled, he's more like a gangly teenager than a seasoned lover even into his forties and fifties. He's energetic, creative, and fun, but totally unconcerned with your pleasure. Coupled with his frequent thoughtless remarks about other girls he's been with, your flabby thighs, or lack of skill at fellatio, the Sagittarius male can really kill the mood.

He prefers sex to be free of emotions and restraints; it's one of the many reasons he's so likely to cheat. He can't stand an emotionally needy or insecure woman, and he detests the "commitment" aspect of sexual relations. According to him, sex is an act that should be enjoyed for what it is, and it's become far too big of a deal in contemporary society. It should be easy; after all, it's just two or more people getting together to enjoy being human. Right? And there are so many ways that sex can be enjoyed, it's one of the few bodily functions that he'll never get bored with. He's into foreplay, role playing, games, exhibitionism—generally, anything that will keep him entertained. His partner is little more than a doll with which he can explore his own sensations. He has no concept of making love to her. For the less-evolved Sagittarius, everything he does in the bedroom centers on himself. As far as he's concerned, he is the only real person that's a part of the act. If he doesn't carefully nurture his relationships—both sexual and platonic—then he can easily forget that there is a world outside of himself with people that have feelings too.

An added irony to the Sagittarius's sexuality is his tendency to embrace religion or philosophy with much fervor and more than a few loopholes. While he may believe in traditional households and marriages, he's kissed another guy more than once and in more than one place. And while he may embrace abstinence, he could be a compulsive exhibitionistic masturbator. He has a definite belief system about sex, and while it might not fit neatly into a definition, you can bet he has it figured out.

Preferred Games

The Try Anything Once Guy

Homosexuality, sadomasochism, submissive-dominant, dressing like a Swedish milkmaid, you name it, he's willing to try it. He needs to be perpetually entertained, and he's open to new experiences and people—maybe a little *too* open for some of his lovers. All too often, trying anything once becomes trying anyone once, especially if he lacks self-control or has been spoiled by women in the past.

In It for the Chase

He's a rambunctious sort whose only request from life is that it be fun, and there are few things more entertaining for a Sagittarius than chasing women. It's one of the few things that keep his attention, but a woman must be very skilled at her part in the game. She must not let him get too close for too long, nor should she appear unattainable. Above all, she must be fun and know how to hold onto a man without him realizing it.

Just a Touch Idealistic

The Sagittarius can fall heavily into religious dogma, imposing his ideals on the world around him and becoming furious when everything and everyone seems to fall short. He firmly believes that good people act a certain way, and if his lover does anything he considers immoral, depraved, or weak, he's more likely to dump her in the gutter than give her a helping hand to the closest rehab center. This becomes a tricky matter when he requires her to shed her hesitancy about certain unusual sexual acts. After all, he might later turn against her for being too free with herself.

God's Gift to Women

He expects to be pleased. He had better be pleased; although he himself may be all quantity and no quality when it comes to sex, his partner had better be well skilled in the bedroom arts. He doesn't really care if she gets off, as long as he does, and he doesn't mind telling her about how much better his last lover was in comparison. When he's in this mood, women are little more than holes to penetrate and he dislikes being reminded that they have such things as thoughts and feelings of their own.

The Idolater

He's absolutely convinced that the object of his affection is the most perfect person in the world. His ego, his life, his entire being is caught up in her and their relationship. He abandons his independence and wraps himself in the chains of love, even throwing himself into marriage before coming to his senses. This game can keep him entranced for minutes, years, or decades depending on the ability of his subject to keep up her appearance of perfection.

What He Needs to Learn About Sex

If his many partners could take a vote, they'd likely agree that what he needs first and foremost is tact. Being emotionally distant and physically promiscuous is one thing. Letting one's partner know about both in a sterile, indifferent manner is something else entirely. His inability to see his actions from his partner's perspective can also lead to harsh realities being thrust upon her, and his remorselessness doesn't help. He should put more effort into emotional ties and stop seeing women as traps waiting to snatch his independence away.

What You Need to Know About
a *Sagittarius* Woman

November 22–December 21

Clothes strewn around the room, naked before you knew what her intentions were, she presses herself against you and reaches for your crotch. She ignores your hesitation and arches backward, driving her hips into you and letting the light play on her athletic neck and firm breasts. You caress her boldly. Instead of demurring as you expect, she nearly purrs with approval and need. You flip her onto her knees, her back pressed against your chest. Without preamble, you enter her, and she begins to work herself. Delighted by her freedom, you let yourself go. As the woman of your dreams would, she is always ready and willing, until dawn breaks across the sky and she gathers up her clothes. Whether you'll ever see her again, you don't know. Dreams have a tendency not to last.

The Privileged Daughter of the God of All Gods

The planet Jupiter has an interesting and mysterious history. Some astronomers believe Jupiter was the sun in its own universe long ago. Even today it forms its own mini-universe with its four planet-sized moons. The Sagittarius woman also has a mysterious history, one she never shares with contemporary friends and which she never forgets herself. Each Sagittarius woman is solidly built on her previous selves, and each era in her life is a grand adventure with a different goal. Having learned much, she transforms into a new self and moves on to the next stage, the next journey.

Mythologically speaking, Jupiter (Zeus, in the Greek pantheon) decided to steal his dad's universe rather than make a new one for himself, and so, too, the Sagittarius seeks to mold what is already there rather than look for something new. She works within the current social standards, customs, and practices, and revolutionizes them to a freer and more equal way of thinking. Most often the Sagittarius is the mother who has a full-time job rather than the woman who rejects the role of mother or wife and seeks a life of solitary economic comfort. As our society become more accepting of women outside of their traditional roles, the Sagittarius woman will be more comfortable expanding her own.

Metis, the goddess of prudence and wisdom, was Jupiter's first wife and she is always the first trait of the Sagittarius woman to be noticed. And just as Metis tried in vain to avoid Jupiter at first, the Sagittarius's own prudence is remarkably hit or miss until she is well into her thirties. Of course, Jupiter's many indiscretions showed his first marriage to be short-lived indeed, and the Sagittarius female isn't known for her monogamy either. She tries hard to be the ideal wife and mother, though. Centaurs, known for their wisdom and healing arts, and their libido, were created by Jupiter and are the symbol of Sagittarius.

Her Top Traits Explored

She's Prudent

Prudence is the characteristic often used to describe a Sagittarius woman. It may be a surprise that this energetic, adventurous woman's main trait is such a down-to-earth one, but all of her eccentricities are based in *this* reality, on *this* planet, during *this* time and with *these* people. She's idealistic and has difficulty accepting the harsher realities of life (a tendency which can later flip-flop into disillusionment about the human condition and fatalism). However, she isn't blind to them.

She chooses her partners for their financial success and stability, her house for its comfort and style, her wardrobe to show off her figure, and her children to show off her feminine prowess. Her career is designed to lead and control. Even if she isn't a CEO, she'll always be in charge of something vital to the company. While she's just as adventurous as her male counterpart, she's much more discreet with her deviations and indiscretions. She's a private person who somehow makes everyone think she's their best friend, and her energy and attention to detail make her an endearing and fun companion.

Sexually, she's freer than you think. Once the bedroom doors are closed, anything goes, and her stamina and creativity can make a car bomb outside go off without notice by either her or her partner. As for her fidelity, it depends on the situation as it does with all prudent people. If she's married, there's a good chance her affairs will only be emotional. If she doesn't believe that the prospects for a long-term, mutually beneficial relationship are good, she has no problem showering her attention on others.

She's Independent

Few women are as capable of functioning on their own as a Sagittarius woman is. She's even more independent than the male Sag, who tends to attach himself emotionally and egotistically to his long-term partners. The Sagittarius female approaches each relationship with detached intellectualism and an understanding that she is intrinsically neither more nor less with her partner than without. Even so, she may rationalize that commitment provides materialistic stability and other added benefits. Intellectualizing the situation is her primary defense when it comes to her heart, which is quite soft once the tough outer layers and random streaks of hilarity are stripped away.

When involved, the Sagittarius woman is hesitant to put restraints on her lover. She allows him enough rope to hang himself. She expects the same leverage herself and won't welcome any clutching, suspicion, stalking, or clinging. She's on this planet to have a good time and to experience the world and learn what it has to teach her. She isn't here for drama or to be tied down by a jealous partner.

Sexual independence can be both a good and a bad thing. On the one hand, she's capable of pleasing herself and she isn't shy about doing whatever it will take. On the other hand, she isn't emotionally involved in her lovemaking and sex with her will most often feel like two people getting together for a good time, and not a "this is the love of my life and fireworks are cascading around us" phenomenon. Her understanding of human motivations and desires and her appreciation for the pleasure sex can bring makes her more understanding of her partner's attention to other women (as long as the Sagittarius woman never finds out that he's gone any further than fantasizing and flirting).

She's High Energy

Everywhere she goes, high voltage follows. She's the busiest person you've ever met, and her brain never seems to stop working. Multitasking is second nature to her, and it allows her to grab as big a hold on life and adventure as she can without wasting any time or opportunity. She lives to move and finds joy in her body and the body of her lover. She knows how to vibrate her aura in order to enliven those around her, propelling their auras to become high energy, as well. This has a negative effect of leaving those around her "addicted" to her energy. They drain her electricity and conserve their own.

Because she moves so fast and seems to be everywhere at once, it's hard to get her to sit down and really focus on a single thing, especially if it's something that doesn't directly pertain to her. This can be especially difficult for her partners, who may take her self-interested nature as selfishness, in general, and never think that she expects them to do the same with their own interests. She doesn't understand the concept of unity with another human. The closest she comes to it is companionship. She fears needing another person and tries to keep herself from falling in love until her rational brain has looked at all the factors—financial stability, emotional maturity, etc.—and given the okay.

Sexually, her high energy pays off and she usually outlasts her partner in bed. To the Sagittarius, sex is an *experience* that needs to be explored and savored for the simple act that it is and the fact that it represents life. She doesn't bring her emotions into the bedroom unless she's angry, in which case hard, rough sex is on the menu. Monogamy is a rational possibility, and the Sagittarius woman understands that it'll probably be the least abrasive course in the end. None the less, her body screams for random, manly partners and her energy makes her more than capable of entertaining many partners at once.

Sex with a Sagittarius Female

She's more than capable of being a sex goddess, but there's something totally detached about her lovemaking that keeps her from ever being termed truly seductive or passionate. Even on those rare occasions when she's completely focused on you for an entire night, expecting an encore the next night has a greater chance of leaving you with a firm lecture about the value of respecting her independence than a second round of mind-numbing sex.

She understands the animal-lust side of sex and can give herself completely to the act without any inhibitions. Many of her partners find this kind of no-strings-attached sex exhilarating—at first. Then they get frustrated when the relationship doesn't seem to ever move past it. This lack of traditional commitment can make some men uncomfortable, and the Sagittarius woman does better with equally independent and free-spirited partners than with someone who's clingy and demanding. For some Sagittarius women, sex is the only "intimate" act in their partnerships. Even with a long-term relationship, they are more likely to have a friendship with plenty of freedom on both sides than anything resembling romance.

In sex, she allows herself freedom of expression. In emotional situations, she often overintellectualizes her feelings and those of her partner, rationalizing or even dismissing feelings as soon as she has ferreted out their root causes. She is not comfortable with vulnerability and demands equality with or domination over her partner in her relationships. Although she can be a die-hard humanitarian who seeks to help others better their situations, the truth is: she's most comfortable with people whom she perceives are lesser than herself because she'd rather not have to fight for position. This can give a patronizing air to her relationships and put her in the caretaker's role, which further removes her emotionally.

The Sagittarius woman prefers sex to be untamed, wild, natural, and joyous. She exults in her body and the sensations it has, and she honestly enjoys the bodies of others. She's not one for staged affairs with rose petals and candles. She prefers spontaneity in her lovemaking. When the rest of her life becomes stagnant, this area will suffer as well and possibly even lead her to remove herself from the joy of living and of her body, leaving her an empty shell.

Preferred Games

The Utilitarian

You have male parts, she has female parts and there's a reason why they fit so well together. Even the gay Sagittarius is able to fit quite nicely into her female partner. Sex has a function, which is to feel good and to create life (not only by making babies, but by reminding people that they are *alive*)—and sex should be enjoyed without unnecessary restriction. It has nothing to do with who you are or who she is or what emotions are between you.

The Mother, Nursemaid, and Wife

Despite her drum being thrummed to a different tune, the Sagittarius woman tries so hard to live in the traditional woman's role, but even this she somehow turns into a feminist soap box. At first, the game is innocent, and she honestly wants to be the submissive caretaker, but it evolves to a means of ensuring dominance over her mate and home. Taking care of another implies you are more able either physically, mentally, or emotionally than they are, and this woman feels most comfortable when her dominance is unquestioned. If she gets into a power struggle, she'd rather quit the game.

The Gilded Cage

For someone so remarkably intelligent, she has a tendency to fall for charm and empty promises. In her more reckless years, she likely flitted from one romance to another, always looking for the better deal, the one with more adventure and freedom. Eventually, she realizes that she's painted herself into a corner, and that those who tend to promise her the most freedom offer her the least. Even choosing the single life has its limitations. Reality of life is that in making one choice, other possibilities are lost.

Her Inner Rabbit

She can screw like there's no tomorrow. Half the time it seems as though she doesn't mind if the object of her attentions is man, woman, or the random piece of furniture. The other half of the time, she'll jump it or them, him or her, even if she does mind, just for the hell of it. Outside or inside, public or private, she's not an exhibitionist. She just enjoys spontaneity and frequency. Sex is natural and wonderful for the mind and body.

The Straight Shooter

When she sees what she wants, she goes after it without hesitance, remorse, or tact. When she's confident in her committed relationship, she lets everyone know about her future marriage—even if her future husband has no immediate plans of proposing. Her flirtations are full of poorly concealed innuendos, and she's much more likely to initiate sex than she is to wait for an invitation. It's difficult to know exactly what she thinks, be it good or bad. It's the only thing about her that no one has ever been able to pin down.

What She Needs to Learn About Sex

Not only can sex be a celebration of life, it can also be the ultimate union of two people and not just for the sake of getting one another off. If she would allow herself to be vulnerable and to accept and nurture vulnerability in her partner without seeing it as weakness, she would be able to experience the joys of true partnership, and she would learn that trust is what holds her to her partner and not necessity or an inability to be independent. Trust can be had without monogamy or boredom if that's what she's worried about.

Capricorn

What You Need to Know About
a *Capricorn* Man

December 22–January 20

He's told you before that to him sex is not knowing where you end and where he begins, and you're surprised that a man who is so self-contained allows his body to mesh with another's so completely. In fact, you've learned to pay careful attention to the small things with him: a glance, a touch, a shift in stance, because each speaks volumes about what he's feeling. You know that talk is cheap and these little clues provide infinitely more comfort than a thousand words. The simple kindnesses he gives you prove his feelings well enough, for when he fills you, he looks into your eyes and you know that you fill him just as completely.

Saturn, the Deposed King

Commander of the old holy order, Saturn ruled during the Golden Age of man, when all was a utopia and man was still pure. Eventually, Saturn was dethroned by his son, Jupiter (Zeus in Greek mythology) and man sank to the folly and hedonism personified by Jupiter's many lusts and his desire for vengeance. The Capricorn himself always has the air of a man eternally stuck in the good old days. He's aware of the destructive changes men have wrought on themselves. Still, he tries to maintain some of the original purity of the race of mankind by adhering to traditional values. The Capricorn male clings to his beliefs while he maintains a stoic, detached exterior. He reacts to his patron's fall from favor by retaining some grace and attempting to achieve a measure of respect for himself through social and economic positions.

In astrology, Saturn governs self-control, responsibility, and the "thou shall not's" of life. The Capricorn male is not so much born to rule as he is a man who has already ruled and is having one hell of a time giving up the leadership position. In an effort to do so, he may become overly judgmental of others, or overly lax in his self-control, and resort to drugs and alcohol to help him relax his need to dominate a situation, or even as tools for subversively doing so. Saturn himself, out of fear that he'd lose his authority, ate his children as soon as they were born to ensure they could not fulfill the prophesy that one of them would take his throne. When Jupiter attempted to do just that, such a war ensued as to nearly destroy the world. And, as many exiled rulers are, Saturn became the scapegoat for everything that was wrong, while Jupiter, the new ruler, was heralded as the perfect king.

His Top Traits Explored

He's Repressed

The sign of Capricorn stands for any pursuit that takes a great deal of time to reach fruition, as well as for restriction, self-control, and social status. The Capricorn male faces a lifelong struggle with his excessive tendencies as he tries to package his larger-than-life personality into a more conventional bread box to make it easier for himself and others to handle.

As a somewhat pessimistic fatalist, the Capricorn male leans toward self-indulgence, especially of illegal substances and sexual affairs. (After all, what's the point of being so self-controlled if there's nothing there that needs to be controlled?) It's uncomfortably easy for him to talk himself into betraying his lover or his health by reminding himself that everything's bound to end anyway, regardless of what he does at any particular moment. However, he could not be a Capricorn without rigid self-regulation, and in an attempt to control his raunchier cravings, many Capricorn men have a tendency to become fanatical followers of religion or societal traditions. Part of him believes that women were made to take care of men and that it is his lover's job to make sure his home life is as comfortable and secure as possible, regardless of his extramarital activities.

His fluctuation between steely repression and melting self-indulgence is a trademark of his sexual expressiveness in the bedroom. His sudden passions are followed by long periods of detachment. In a way, his abstinence is a means of penance for his previous hot and heavy behavior, either because his religious attitudes make him feel guilty or because he's scared himself with his inhibitions and the power of his lust for a woman. If his partner becomes resentful over this ebb and flow, he's likely to take his sexual attentions elsewhere, letting her deal with one side of his personality, and his mistress to deal with the other.

There's also a certain kinkiness hidden in the Capricorn's personality. It doesn't have to do with various positions or exotic accoutrements. It has more to do with playing a few taboo masculine roles, such as simulating rape or incest, playing high priest or dark official during sexual religious rites, or having sex with multiple women or prostitutes at the same time. Again, what's the point of repression if there's nothing to repress?

He's Emotionally Aloof

Does he want a relationship or not? Is he interested in you sexually? Is he in love or does he just barely tolerate you? It's hard to tell with this stoic man. Although it's tough to see on the surface, he *does* have feelings—quite a lot of them, actually, and they all run deep. His heart is remarkably fragile and when he falls in love, he does so with such abandon that it terrifies him. There's a good chance that the object of his affection knows little about his feelings for her, though.

One of the reasons for his lack of demonstrativeness is that he's always holding out for something better to come along and he doesn't want to make any commitment before he's sure that his lover is as good as he'll get. He enjoys the freedom of being able to move from one woman to another, even if it tears him apart. Being born under the sign of repression means that he's continually fluctuating between extravagant displays and total emotional detachment.

In order to find out how this man is feeling, it will probably be necessary to poll the people closest to him, and you can expect to get a small piece of the puzzle from each. He'll only rarely tell you outright and any attempt to force it out of him will be met either by withdrawal or with an explosion of anger. Even after sex, his emotions are difficult to determine, and he's one of those men who will talk about a previous relationship more than his current one without any regard as to which is more important or dedicated.

He's Practical

Each action is carefully thought out and every consequence examined in each facet. The Capricorn male is rational and practical, and his life is measured and ambitious. His extreme practicality is a method of hiding his sometimes bizarre inner life and it also serves as a way to minimize the effects of his impulsive tendencies, which can devastate his finances and relationships.

Measuring every quality of his lover before forming any commitments can be a blow to his partner's pride. It is, however, a habitual Capricorn trademark. When he does commit, it's with the understanding that he'll leave if someone better comes along. Often, he attempts to soften the impact of this by telling his partner that she has the same option. The perpetual social climber, he prefers to marry for money and status rather than love. If he does stumble upon the embodiment of his ideals (usually someone naive and wholesome), he'll be willing to lessen the financial expectations somewhat—especially if his own situation is stable.

Although his approach to sex is practical, he has more than the normal amount of fetishes and far-out fantasies. His practical nature gets in the way of his sexual expression as he is bound by what he feels he is and is not allowed to do in bed. Eventually, this unspent energy has to go somewhere. He'll either find himself in another woman's bed or drowning in substance abuse. His traditional mindset, the prescribed roles for women, and his all-important social standing all link together to make it nearly impossible for him to find a mate who's as in to unusual sex as he is. He's infinitely happier if he's able to make such a connection, though.

Sex with a Capricorn Male

This man is more than likely extremely good in bed. When not engaged in his aforementioned kinkier acts, he likes straight sex without the frills, or so it seems on the surface, anyway. He has some naughtier inclinations that he might not feel comfortable having satisfied by the "traditional" woman he's chosen to partner with. (Doing so would detract from her wholesome appearance.) He enjoys pleasuring his partner and taking firm command of her body. Capricorns tend to be born with the sexual knowledge of an experienced middle-aged man. As long as he isn't one of those deeply repressed or traditional Capricorns who tends to expect his partner to please or stimulate him rather than doing any of the work himself, he will take most of the accountability for the caliber of the sex in his relationships, using his ability to delay his own orgasms to both his and his partner's advantage.

He's often attracted to other men because they possess qualities he wishes he had himself. With his general confusion about the metaphysics of sex, he can turn this attraction or appreciation into sexual energy, wishing to be a part of the other man through sexual means in order to somehow share in his glory. Because of his typically traditional values, such feelings can leave him traumatized and distraught about his masculinity, and drive him to pursue ever more female conquests or religious purifications.

It's rare for the Capricorn to have a sexual experience that isn't well thought out beforehand. Even his affairs are planned. Because sex has a lot of traditional and religious meanings, the Capricorn male cannot and will not take it lightly, even though he may take his relationships for granted. For this reason, sex with him can feel like a solemn event, full of dark looks and ritualism and lacking in any positive or joyous emotion. When his oppressive air is coupled with his tendency to cheat, the Capricorn's worst enemy is himself, and his partners have a high risk of suffering negative emotional consequences simply for being involved with him.

Preferred Games

The Metrosexual

He knows how to dress to play his role to its best advantage. His shirt, pants, shoes, and woman are all in style and look fabulous draped around him. He's desperately interested in social status, and seeks ways of outdoing every other man in the room, although he doesn't really take the competition from women very seriously. Everything is designed and arranged to best suit him and his ambitions, and he isn't afraid to marry purely for money or status.

The Zealot

Whichever religion he chooses—probably the most popular one in his area—he's absolutely certain of its truth. He brings piety to a new level, and you'll find him in church whenever they'll let him in. Religion gives him a ready-made list of rules and restrictions, an explanation for why each and every one of them is necessary, and what to do to absolve himself of any indiscretion he commits. He won't always stick to the sexual rules prescribed to him, but he will at least feel guilty each time he violates them.

The Man

He's the man, and that means he's in charge. He's the breadwinner, wears the pants in the family, and makes all the major decisions. He can be as stubborn as an unruly child when he doesn't get his way, and he actually stomps his foot and pouts, perhaps even knocking over a few plates, until you give in. He firmly believes that women are scatterbrained, petty, catty, childlike people who are there for his pleasure and should come and go at his command. He can be persuaded by them, sure, but only because he enjoys spoiling them and making them giggle. The truth is that he doesn't like competition and by undermining over half the population, he removes over half of his challengers.

The Master

As already noted, the Capricorn male loves being in charge and some of his favorite sexual fantasies involve playing the masculine role in some inappropriate sexual situation. He loves being in full control of his partner and having her either obey his every command or be in a scenario where she has no choice but to acquiesce, such as blindfolded and gagged. When he plays with BDSM, there are no safe words involved. Playing with experienced, "well worn" women makes these games easier in the end, and he isn't above hiring help.

The Corrupter

Few things meet his egotistical, misogynistic needs like corrupting someone who already has higher status and is purer of thought and body. He enjoys wealthy, naïve women to whom he can introduce sex, drugs, and the dark side of society. Orchestrating an aristocrat's fall from grace and being the maestro of her descent is intoxicating for him and helps affirm some of his beliefs that women should act as he thinks they should, or suffer the consequences.

What He Needs to Learn About Sex

Mr. Capricorn needs to find a means of strengthening his confidence out of the bedroom before he decides to bring his ego into bed with him. His traditional views of women can place undue restriction on both him and his partner, and true emotional fulfillment in a relationship occurs when both people are equal and equally appreciated. He would also benefit from learning how to experience joy in sex. Meditation and concentration on physical sensations rather than intellectual consequences could help him here, especially if the exercises are done with a partner he respects and cherishes.

What You Need to Know About
a *Capricorn* Woman

December 22–January 20

The longer you know her, the more incredible she is in bed. As the bond grows deeper, she's more comfortable showing you her sexual side, and you're both thrilled and nervous about what you find. She's the most demanding lover you've ever been with, but you're glad she challenges you because it keeps your interest and brings both of you to new sexual heights. Sex is a methodical process, but without any of the staleness that implies. Instead, sex with this woman is like watching a flower blossom again and again. First, the bud ripens and grows. Then it unfolds. Finally, a lovely bloom lies before you.

Saturn, the Deposed King

Saturn, the ruler of restriction and responsibility, was at one time ruler of the universe before being dethroned by his son Jupiter. The Capricorn female is less troubled by her patron's downfall than the Capricorn male is, and she doesn't take it as personally. A perpetual politician herself, she has an inner confidence that stems in part from pride over her ruling planet's accomplishments and prestige. She knows she comes from good stock even if her earthly parents were less than estimable.

Just as the exiled Saturn came to earth and began the Golden Age of mankind where the world was a utopia and men were immortal, the Capricorn female will go through at least one major shift of position in her life, and her friends will have difficulty reconciling the girl they know and love with the one she used to be or is becoming. While Saturn's loss of power came after a war with Jupiter that nearly destroyed the universe, the Capricorn woman's own change will probably be less dramatic but no less thorough and it might cost her more than a few friends.

Saturn is not an easy planet to live under. He's demanding and likes to test his disciples to see if they are worthy of the extraordinary gifts he can give them: financial luxury, self-confidence, and the ability to direct their own lives. The Capricorn woman does not have an easy life and is often faced with one disaster after the other until she is all but exhausted. She does, however, have the strength of character that only comes from being sorely tested and making it through better than how she went in. She accepts fate and honestly tries to live with as much integrity as possible. Her battle with trauma, though, makes security very important to her and very difficult to find.

Her Top Traits Explored

She's Pragmatic

Perhaps due to the socialization of women to work within "accepted" confines (i.e., lower wages, sexism), the Capricorn woman is better able to handle the restrictive nature of her sign than her male counterpart is. She doesn't struggle with the bonds nearly as much as he does. Instead of fighting with herself, she finds a way to achieve her goals by using tradition and responsibility as tools rather than the "captors" many modern women see them as. She doesn't need to break the mold, and most of the time she wouldn't want to. She's comfortable being able to add her own eccentric touches to the finished product.

Every aspect of her life is prioritized, and if she avoids her sign's natural inclination toward depression, the Capricorn woman can become one of the most fulfilled women of the zodiac. While her priorities might not match up with everyone else's, they give her a feeling of pride and accomplishment and help her achieve her goals. She's busy and active, and often better at running everyone else's lives than she is at running her own. This is one woman who lives her life to the fullest, accomplishing as many of her goals as possible and usually one right after the other in a perfectly logical (to her) sequence.

Her approach to sex is very down to earth. She doesn't waste time or energy, and she has a reason behind every move she makes. That doesn't mean she's overly conventional or without any imagination. The Capricorn woman is surprisingly skilled and innovative in bed, and she has the lasting power of a mountain. She has a tendency to be insecure about herself at first, but once paired with a positive, reassuring partner, there is no limit to what she can do and how many times she can do it—as long as it makes sense to her.

She's Eccentric

"Capricious" shares the same root as "Capricorn" with good reason, and "kinky" is synonymous with "capricious" for more than just the hell of it. Despite being notoriously traditional, the Capricorn woman is one of the consummate oddballs of the zodiac, often forsaking traditional ways for very non-traditional ones. She is who she is *because* of her unique rebellion against the norms of society. While she can do a great number of strange things inside and with the box, she never manages to think *outside* of it.

Of course, whatever she does is perfectly rational from her point of view, and she has a good reason for all of it. Her reasons might not be understandable to those around her, though, which is both a source of insecurity and, eventually, inner strength. Her tendency to keep her cards close to her chest doesn't make this trait any easier for those close to her to handle.

However, she tends to make up for her unusual nature in the bedroom. Her eccentricity and ability to do many things with traditional sex make her one hell of a lover. While her kinkiness isn't too pronounced, even with a trusted partner, she has awe-inspiring endurance and an almost compulsive libido. She learns early on the joys and political aspects of sex, and her enjoyment of it depends on her partner and how accepting he is of female virility.

She's Insecure

The Capricorn woman's insecurity stems from a discrepancy between her inner life and her outer one. Inwardly, the Capricorn woman may feel more than capable of being a CEO or CFO of a major Fortune 500 company while, outwardly, she gets nervous balancing her checkbook. Outwardly, she may be firmly entrenched in the upper-middle class while, inwardly, she's living on the street and barely surviving. In either case, there's a difference between how she's really doing and how she feels she's doing, and how close the latter comes to the reality of the former depends on the Capricorn woman's self-esteem and self-confidence. Many Capricorn women try to find partners who compensate for their own lack of confidence, or who can insulate them from their inner feelings. However, the Capricorn woman will never be truly secure until she finds confidence in herself and for herself.

She gets nervous about having sex. She's afraid of the difference between what society expects of her and what she feels inside. She's terrified of falling in love and having to depend on someone who might let her down and ruin all of her carefully laid plans. And most people will never know she feels any of it. She learned early on that the best defense for insecurity is putting on the front of total confidence, and she clings to the mask with both fists, sometimes digging her nails in when things get overwhelming—despite the pain. As many insecure people do, she may turn to substances, including alcohol and psychiatric quick fixes, to push her beyond her nervousness and reveal the outgoing, confident woman she is inside.

Sex with the Capricorn Female

She's not one of those brainless types who flirts incessantly and turns out to be a cold fish in bed. While she does flirt, she's both more straightforward and more innocent about it, and she never promises anyone more than she's willing to deliver, just in case her bluff is called and humiliation follows. When she learns how to be relaxed about herself and her body, and if she manages to pair up with an accepting partner, this woman's sex drive could melt the Alps. She's fully able to embrace the sensations in her body and often either becomes multi-orgasmic or else her first and only orgasm gives her such a quake as to lay her and her partner flat for hours.

For a woman who doesn't usually mature until she's past forty, her younger years are often characterized by bad relationships, nearly disabling shyness, and a major dissonance she feels deep within herself. While she struggles to find the most comfortable fit, she's likely to force herself into unnatural positions, like committing to an unambitious loser, a drug addict, or someone emotionally and physically cold. After such experiences, her sexuality is often bottled up and hidden to avoid embarrassment or pain. It may take her quite some time to undo all the knots she has tied herself in.

Capricorn women are generally more comfortable in committed relationships, and prefer men who are stable and will provide them with security. The Capricorn woman must respect her partner, and he must be able to take command of himself and his life. She wants to be coddled and protected at the same time that she demands her lover to be strong and unwilling to submit easily. There's a certain point with some independent people where they wish someone else—someone more than worthy—could take control for a moment or two and let them rest, and the Capricorn woman is no exception. This issue plays out sexually where the Capricorn woman is more than willing to take command of her lover but secretly hopes that he'll have the right combination of a demanding presence, extraordinary skill, and tactful manners to do so without infringing on her independence or control. She's a woman that can only be mastered by a master and there are, unfortunately, so few of those around.

She is more comfortable having sex while in a committed relationship than having a bunch of one-night stands. Once over her initial knee-jerk response of finding commitment and security *now* rather than waiting for the *right* partner to come along, she looks for a man who's financially stable, of good social standing, and tenacious in the business world.

Preferred Games

The Heiress

She's of the right lineage, she can have anything she wants and, damn it, she's the best woman in the world, no matter what anyone else thinks. She might as well walk around with a tiara and scepter. To say she puts on airs is an understatement on a grand scale. Unless a person is either pompous himself or able to see through her ruse to the insecurity behind, this Capricorn game intimidates everyone and may leave her a lonely, self-exiled princess with only her insufferable self as company.

She's All About the Patience

The Capricorn woman can wait a long time to achieve a goal. Setting down each detail needed to achieve what she wants can look to others like she's not doing much of anything, until all of a sudden she has everything that she wanted from life. Likewise, her patience is a key part to her lovemaking, as she thinks just about any sexual act or romance should *take time*. While studying the ground for potholes, pitfalls, and rough shoulders is a painstaking job no matter how much practice you have at it, she needs to feel that she has firm footing with each step she takes.

The Bra-burning Antithesis of Traditional Woman

This is a total reversal of her compulsion to accept traditional values and is usually a result of the Capricorn coming to terms with herself and gaining a lot of confidence as well. She's a strong, capable, and ambitious woman, and she will decide for herself what she wants from life. She isn't afraid of making the first move sexually or romantically, and she may even allow her sexuality to lead her to many different beds with all the reckless joy of a wild horse escaping confinement. She is happy if, albeit, a little less "safe."

Romantic

She wants to be wooed and romanced and swept off her feet by some charismatic, successful man with a bold, almost wild, streak. She wants a man who'll take care of her and coddle her for the rest of her life, someone who'll challenge her and love her for her strength of mind. She wants to be treated with the utmost respect at all times, but she hardly wants a man she can trample on. She wants her equal, and in him, a man who anticipates her every desire and sees that she's worth the trouble.

The Sexual Obstacle Course

The Capricorn woman demands a lot from her partners. Loyalty, respectability, and financial success are only some of her requirements. She also insists on virility, manliness, above-average IQ, and the ability to make her mouth water and her muscles turn to jelly. She has some specific ideas about how a man needs to have sex with her, and it has little to do with his needs. Being able to enjoy sex with her lover is of paramount importance, and if a man fails here, he had better overcompensate in other

areas or the Capricorn woman will find someone more quali-
fied to be her partner.

What She Needs to Learn About Sex

She needs to love herself no matter what others think or how
they treat her, and she needs to gain real self-respect and not
affectations. She also needs to love her body and the joy it can
bring her. The Capricorn woman's grounded stability isn't im-
mune from earthquakes and rather than dreading the next one,
she needs to learn how to inoculate herself from the worst of
its possible effects and then to strive to find meaning and passion
in every day, so that when the end comes she can truly say that
she lived well.

Aquarius

What You Need to Know About
an *Aquarius* Man

January 21–February 19

The candles on the altar are dimly reflected in his eyes, and you feel him embracing you in double warmth. Smoke from the incense dances slowly around your entwined limbs, flirting with the texture of your skin and overlapping the sweet, ancient smell that is sex. He is never lost in the act, except perhaps at the moment of climax, when he finally surrenders to the power that has been cultivated and harvested with such ritual exactness. It is that power and no simple physical sensation that combines your souls and launches them in tandem.

Uranus, God of the Sky and Lofty Ideals

Uranus, the god of all Aquarians, was once the god of all gods. Both the son and the husband of Gaia—Mother Earth—Uranus was the god of the sky. He fathered the Titans and the giants and caused his wife so much pain when he tried to hide his atrocities within her that she had her son Saturn, who himself would eventually be dethroned, castrate Uranus. True, there have been other gods who were dethroned. The previously mentioned dethronement of Saturn at the hands of his son Jupiter is an example. However, Uranus is one of the few gods who were castrated. Gaia wanted Uranus castrated so he'd stop fathering monsters and because he hurt her. What this does to the Aquarius is up to speculation (usually by the Aquarius), but it is apparent to anyone who has met an Aquarius and listened to his dogma, the "children" of his mind. Not surprisingly, the Aquarius male is dealt a further blow because his sub-ruler is Saturn. The double dethronement of his two chief gods eats away at the Aquarius, who feels robbed of his proper place among the royalty of Olympus and, therefore, unceasingly looks for a way to break into the Aquarian kingdom and claim his true title. Another result of his gods' exile is that the Aquarius has learned a few valuable lessons about how to remove others from power, whether they think they are his friend or family. He is typically involved in a stiff rivalry with some authority sometime in his life, either a father or brother, and he doesn't appreciate women who are more intelligent than he is himself. He'll never be with someone stupid, though. He isn't exactly "attentive" to his spouse either, as Uranus showed in his treatment of Gaia. Uranus's dethronement and the method of his downfall may be seen as not only a removal from political power, but from masculinity—an issue that haunts the Aquarius.

His Top Traits Explored

He's Spiritual

The Aquarius male is more interested than most in spirituality, although a great deal more of his interest lies in religion's ability to control and set rules for others than in what happens after death—unless whatever occurs beyond the veil will lead him to an even more powerful position. His interest in the meaning of life is usually more of an interest in how to beat the game of life than in how to progress as a human, especially if such progress would require a revoking of power. He tends to flit from one religion to another, trying to find the one that will give him the most power. More than anything, he wishes to wield the power of life and death over others and to command them to do as he says. Smiting his enemies is a typical fantasy of his, and he spends much of his time trying to find mystical means of doing so. While on an intellectual level he believes in the power of persuasion and understands that belief and the human mind are responsible for most miracles, he hopes that there is more to it and that true magical power actually exists and that one day he will find it.

The Aquarian, in particular, is likely to use spirituality to secure for himself as many bed partners as possible. Introducing a woman to paganism and quickly ushering her into "sex magic" is a common ruse, as is using his position as leader or high priest of a religious tradition. It's a position he lusts for in order to gain access to people who are more likely to succumb to his game than others.

He's Intellectual

The Aquarius is one man who's always stuck in his head. He's ambitious, and doesn't allow anything to get in the way of achieving his goals. His cold, calculating treatment of those around him has earned him an astrological reputation of being an emotionally detached, ladder-climbing, power-seeking man—a man who doesn't care for the people he hurts in the process of attaining his aspirations.

His ability to assess situations and manipulate them for his own benefit can get in the way of his spiritual endeavors, and even though he may truly be religious, his understanding of the monetary and physical benefits it may afford him may appear to discredit his zeal. Similarly, he may truly love someone, but his assessment of their inherited wealth and status (Aquarians are always attracted to the wealthy as they equate money with power) may seem to cheapen his emotions. On the one hand, his ability to seize opportunities will help him gain the life he longs for. On the other hand, he may starve himself and his partner emotionally. It's not that he doesn't *feel*. In fact, his intellect and ambition are controlled mostly by his emotional state. He's just so unaware of his emotions that he would rather suppress them than nurture positive ones. As a result, negative emotions may take hold and leave him with little positive sustenance. This has a huge effect on his sexuality, which remains intellectual and sterile and is seen also as a method of dominance and control. While he may honestly enjoy having sex for the simple joys it brings, he cannot forget who is thrusting into whom, and he may eventually come to see it as his right, just as his wife is often his first disciple and follower (a.k.a. subordinate).

He's Confident

This man didn't have the happiest childhood, nor was adolescence easy on him. The butt of frequent jokes and often out of favor in the political sphere that is high school, the Aquarius male seeks to attain true prestige, and he's certain that he more than deserves it despite whatever effort he himself takes toward his goals. He idolizes those with power, and he firmly believes he has a lot of his own. His relationships are an instrument of his confidence and he expects his mate to be his first, if not most important, backer.

His high ambitions, intellectualism, and lack of hesitancy to use everything for his own gain does not necessarily guarantee him high status in life or much happiness. No matter what pitfalls he encounters, however, he'll always bounce back from them and return stronger than he left—or at least more determined. As far as he is concerned, he is the right one, and he believes that his opinions are a reflection of reality. Those who disagree are just uncomfortable with that reality.

He's sexually confident. At most, he is insecure about his physique but not about his skill, and when he is inclined to have intercourse, he welcomes as much change and excitement as possible. Because his own imagination is somewhat lacking in this area, he doesn't find much opportunity there for power or exercising his mentality.

Sex with an Aquarius Male

Sex is not very important to an Aquarius. He enjoys it, it feels good, but there are far too many strings attached for him to feel comfortable—even if he's the one controlling all the strings. Although sex is not on his list of priorities, he'll notice if it's missing and he'll impulsively need to correct the issue and re-instate his bedroom privileges or find someone else's bedroom to occupy.

The two aspects that this illustrates are (1) his dominance in the relationship, and (2) his "right" to sex. Both are characteristics of his romantic relationships. Whomever he becomes involved with will have the characteristics of a devoted follower.

She must adore him, cherish everything he says and every opinion he has, make sure his every physical need is taken care of, and she'll probably be the one with the stable career so he can pursue his spirituality. The exception to these criteria is when the Aquarius enjoys one-night stands or short-term affairs. In these shorter associations, the Aquarius male finds the best woman around—the most beautiful, accomplished, intelligent, and wealthy—and seduces her simply because she is the best and probably of a higher stratus than he is. The chance of him forming a long-term connection with such a woman isn't high, however, because he prefers looking down at his partner and not up.

While he isn't into extravagant sex, he prefers the down-to-business variety. He is interested in being catered to sexually, and in physically dominating his partner. When he's involved with snobbish ladies, he enjoys lowering them to positions that exaggerate their submission to him (doggy-style, fellatio, and anal sex), and he's not above starting sexual rumors in order to hurt reputations. He isn't opposed to harems and extramarital affairs because he thinks they highlight his masculinity and desirability—two very important topics to him.

Preferred Games

The Standard by Which the World Should Measure Itself

One thing that all Aquarian males firmly believe is that they are supreme examples of the human race and that others should be lucky (or, in the case of disfavor, terrified) to have them around. His opinions aren't "opinions," they are statements of the way the world should be or reflections of how everyone else feels. He's unable to divorce the world from his inner life and is capable of tyrannical rule over others if given the opportunity.

The Media Man

How things appear is of extreme concern to Mr. Aquarius. He's sensitive to any attacks on his authority and will retaliate with as much force and power as he can wield. If dumped, he'll carry out a smear campaign that would put current political commercials to shame, and he can carry a grudge for years. During relationships, he's intent on showing the world how well cared for he is, and how lucky his partner feels to be with him. He'll work hard to embarrass her former lovers and to make his as jealous (and regretful) as possible.

The Guru

He loves the knowledge and power implied in leadership positions and prefers those in religious or spiritual contexts. He feels he knows more than most do about what happens in this world and beyond and is interested in teaching people how to think like he does. Perhaps Jesus Christ being the human embodiment of a deity has given the Aquarius male the idea that religion is the path to mortal and immortal power, but he has difficulty settling for status in the material world alone. When he's playing this game, sex with him is supposed to be considered an honor by his partners, as well as a way of worship.

The Stalker

His tenacity in getting what he wants can cross the line every once in a while. When he sets his sights on a target, he does everything he can in order to ensure that he'll get what he wants, even if that means showing up at your door ten times a day, driving by at night to make sure someone else's car isn't there, or starting rumors about a relationship before there even is one.

The Object of Your Devotion

The one thing he enjoys sexually above all others is being adored and pampered. He wants his lovers to be in awe of him and to feel grateful for his attentions. Outside of the spiritual meaning behind sex with him, he enjoys feeling physically attractive and wants to be desired above all others. Although he rarely shows it, he doesn't have a great deal of confidence in his physical appearance, and he would much appreciate a little reassurance.

What He Needs to Learn About Sex

Other people have feelings and ambitions that might not match his own, and he needs to learn how to deal with it. He might be surprised at how finding an actual partnership rather than a fawning devotee helps him achieve his ambitions in double time and gives him a much needed reality check that will also further his own aims. Learning how to pay attention to and honor his own feelings and those of others will enrich his relationships and ultimately his life.

What You Need to Know About
an *Aquarius* Woman

January 21–February 19

Without warning, she's on top of you, kissing you demandingly and groping as much of you as she can get a hold of. This was the last thing you expected, but you have no doubts how to respond and you enjoy her little surprises. You let her take command of your body, understanding that to reject her now or to lead her in any but the most subtle way would mean that things like this would not happen again in the near future, a blasphemy in miniature. For when she's there, she's very, very there, and when she's gone, she's a vacuum.

Uranus, God of the Sky and Lofty Ideals

The Aquarian woman is far beyond the troubles of her planetary gods. Uranus was god of all gods before being castrated by his son in an effort to keep him from fathering more monster-children with his wife, Gaia (Earth). The Aquarius's sub-ruler, Saturn, was also dethroned by a son, although he was allowed to keep his masculinity. Despite this double dethronement in her astrological lineage, the Aquarius female isn't particularly concerned with either how it reflects on her or what it could mean for her own personality and/or the future. What she has gotten from her Uranus and Saturn patrons is class and a lack of concern for earthly matters.

Uranus is the god of the sky, and Saturn rules organization and restriction. The combined properties of each gives the Aquarian female a distinctly odd personality. She's both independent and tied to her ideals, she's creative and intellectual, while her thoughts and emotions are compartmentalized. A perpetual chained bird, she can only fly so high, but it's still much farther than any of her contemporary humans can. When she has her feathers aligned, when both her planetary ruler and sub-ruler are in a good mood, the two sides of her personality—the creative and the restrained—can help her achieve any goal she desires. Her ability to build a realistic plan to achieve her creative ideals is her greatest asset, and a very powerful one, as well. Unfortunately, bringing lofty goals to earthly realities isn't as easy for her in the romantic realm as in business or academics; her wings often get tangled in her fear of intimacy and she suffers from repressed emotions.

Her Top Traits Explored

She's an Idealist

While the Aquarius male was primarily concerned with power, the female Water Bearer has looked beyond the throne to the place where honor and respectability reside. She has the ability to see through her culture and traditions and envision what the world should be like. She's a unique combination of humanitarian, politician, and accountant. She has the desire to do good for people, the intellect and emotional detachment to realize how good such projects make her look, and the technical ability to see her plans through to the end. While she tries not to infringe on others' beliefs and religiously cultivates an open mind, she has difficulty accepting certain traditions and norms and seeks a way to mesh her idealistic vision with hard reality while remaining out of the spotlight until she's certain of winning a Nobel Prize.

Although her ideals are an integral part of her personality, they also serve as good buffers to real romantic liaisons. It's easy to commit to the perfect person in her head, but much tougher to "give up her freedom" for a real person with real problems. When involved, she distances herself from shows of emotion, because she thinks doing so is a sign of personal weakness, and she resists becoming dependent on her partner. This is where her idealism cuts deep, because it's impossible under such conditions for her earthly romance to equal the one she has in her head. So she tends to widen the gulf between the two to such a point that she eventually ends the relationship on principle. The kicker is that her partner usually has no idea that she's having any problems whatsoever until everything is more than finished and he's handed a filing box and told to clean out his desk. She has been labeled "low-maintenance" by more than a few astrologers. This label is due in a large part to her own somewhat shallow emotional investment in her relationships, and also to her compulsion to keep quiet about whatever's bothering her.

She's in Her Head

Any man looking to woo this airy intellectual had better be well endowed in the brain department. The Aquarius female spends almost all of her time thinking and the rest of it educating herself. Emotions destabilize her cultured quietude and smack her back to earth when all she wants to do is soar and be left alone. Emotions are uncomfortable. Emotions make her say and do things she wasn't planning on and leave her feeling guilty more often than joyous, and she would altogether rather that emotions be gone, or be at least as rational as her thoughts.

It should be no surprise that the Aquarius female tends to end up in relationships with overbearing, possibly even psychologically abusive partners. She requires that her mates be mental heavyweights and yet refuses to get into anything more than a polite discussion on hypotheticals herself, hiding her own strong ideals and allowing herself to be railroaded. Setting standards and learning how to open up and stand up publicly for her beliefs would cure this tendency quickly.

Sexually, she needs to be approached headfirst. She has the most trouble of any sign to get physically turned on unless her brain is taking a large part in the action. Sex with her is always a mind fuck, and she gets a far greater amount of satisfaction out of picking your brain and "rearranging the building blocks" than she does physically, despite how skilled you are in the sack. One trick with her, though, is that no matter how cold she can be, she always benefits the most from a warm, affectionate partner who will eventually teach her to love herself and hopefully to love him in return.

She's Experimental

Open-minded, curious, unconventional, energetic, and intellectual, the Aquarius female brings a hell of a lot to the table, or the four-poster bed. She's exceptionally bright and interested in a great variety of subjects. She gets bored easily, and while she doesn't rely on others to provide stimulus, she prefers her close partners and friends to provide it as long as they're around. She believes that time spent with others is time wasted unless something interesting happens or is discussed. Because so few are tuned to her wavelength, she has difficulty finding companions who are up to par intellectually. She prefers being alone, either mentally or physically, so that she can follow her own inclinations and dream her own dreams.

She's the prime example of how emotions can be divorced from sex. Her emotions never come out in the bedroom. She enjoys her body and her lover's body, but she doesn't see why a biological function should be wrapped in any feelings other than physical ones. Because she doesn't have much emotion for sex, she tends to be indifferent about it. When she does have sex, she wants it to be mentally stimulating and exciting, although she often isn't sure in what ways. A good conversation, an exciting adventure, or learning about something new will always be more important to her than sex. She needs a partner who won't take this lack of interest in sex as a lack of interest in him and who is willing to accept (notice I said "accept" and not "tolerate") her hot and cold sex drive. She can come on strong, swear she's itching for a good tumble, and then push you off in the middle of the third thrust because she suddenly remembered there is something she'd rather be doing. It has nothing to do with your skill; it has everything to do with the temperamental connection between her body and her mind.

Sex with an Aquarius Female

It's a wild ride to be sure, when she's in the mood for it. Sexual interest must come from her brain long before her body is touched, and she never stops thinking. Her main obstacle to achieving an orgasm is that she's concentrating too hard or she can't focus at all. There *must* be something interesting enough to keep her coming back for sex or she will find something better to do with her time. Having a partner bring his ego into the bedroom is a major turnoff, especially when it's used to coerce her into having sex.

When she's ready for a roll in the hay, she'll surprise her lover with her energy and imagination. As long as he doesn't restrict her, as long as he makes sure to give her free rein to explore her sexuality, she'll be happy to have sex—when she wants to. Countering her on this point and demanding sex will only drive her further and further away until she finally disappears completely. She tries very hard to keep emotions away from her sex life, but the vulnerability that comes along with sexual acts—nudity, being penetrated, having her skills judged, etc.—can have either a catastrophic or a miraculous effect on her life and relationships, depending on the sensitivity of her partner. Intimacy doesn't come easily, and may not come at all, for this intellectual woman.

Although she demands excitement in the bedroom, she has strong ideas about what sex should be like and what she is and is not willing to do. She believes in personal dignity and has always been uncomfortable with sexual archetypes, secretly thinking that the woman has the bad end of the bargain and needs to do all that she can to maintain whatever dignity she'll have after "submitting" to the act. If she's a liberated Aquarius, she'll use her sexuality as her personal power base, and she'll do it in such a way as to increase her self-respect. She'll embrace sex as a beautiful, beneficial act, and rob it of its ability to humiliate her. She won't use it as a tool to manipulate or appease. It will be one of the many ways she expresses herself, nothing more, nothing less.

Preferred Games

Promises, Promises

When trying to win a mate, the Aquarian promises a lot more than she's willing to deliver. In her mind, the idea of what may happen between the sheets is often more satisfying than the act itself, and she doesn't understand if her lover gets upset when she doesn't deliver the goods. As soon as she's had the thought, she is on to the next thing and an unfortunately small percentage of her ideas make it to the actual production stage.

What You See

The outer persona of the Aquarius woman doesn't match her inner one. Her forced open-mindedness, her acceptance of those around her, and her ability to match her beliefs to suit those of her company are just ways to keep from revealing her true self to others. She's afraid of rejection and of intimacy. Avoiding disclosure of her ideas and beliefs keeps her from facing either until someone catches the inconsistency between her actions and her words.

It's All in Her Head

The Aquarius female achieves orgasms because she's thought herself into having them or because she has learned to turn off her brain and allow her body sexual release. Either way, her brain is both a major hindrance and a powerful tool for her sexuality. Getting it into the habit of ignoring society's rule and forgetting unskilled or cruel lovers will take some dedication, but it will be well worth it if she does.

The Role-player

With a mind so detached from everything on *this* planet, she prefers being given a task when dealing with other terrestrials so that she can function around them. What this basically means is that she'll do what they expect her to do while the rest of her is off thinking, planning, and generally living a rich inner life that no one else is invited to join. Her Saturn side enjoys a regimented life that is predictable, structured, and safe. Her Uranus side makes her changeable, quirky, and eccentric. Society is more comfortable with her Saturn side, so Saturn takes over her outer demeanor while Uranus has full rein over the interior.

The Submissive

Aquarius women are ultimately drawn to men who can control them. Intellectual thought and mental games feature so prominently in her sex life that it's only natural for her to look for a man who knows how to play them, too. With her ability to differentiate her outer self from her inner self, she's capable of being outwardly submissive while maintaining a well-kept, rich inner world. In fact, she prefers being with someone who controls her outer self because that allows her extra time to spend inside.

What She Needs to Learn About Sex

Sex isn't simply an experience of the body, or of biology, and the intimacy she tries so hard to avoid will actually enrich her life despite the danger it brings. Connecting her mind to her body will double her power as a person and increase her education of the world and all that is in it. Learning how to be comfortable with herself and her beliefs despite the opposition from those around her will also increase her personal power and her enjoyment of life. The ones who turn against her for this are the ones she's better off without, and the ones who stay will be truer than if she had continued concealing herself.

Pisces

What You Need to Know About
a *Pisces* Man

February 20–March 20

He whispers into your ear, "Maybe we should stop. I'm sorry, I got carried away." Feeling his breath makes you shiver. Despite his words, he knows that if he lets you go now, it will be the last time he'll ever touch you. You start to turn away to hide your confusion and embarrassment, but he firmly holds you in place and with one hand lifts your chin, the other wraps around your back and cups your neck as he leans forward and kisses your jaw. You shift your hips forward in an unconscious invitation and find his lips with yours to kiss with equal need.

Neptune in Flux

Around 400 BC, Neptune, a relatively minor Roman god of the sea, began overlapping the Greeks' Poseidon, one of the three rulers of the world (Zeus ruled the heavens, Hades ruled the underworld, Poseidon ruled the oceans, and all three shared the earth). In fact, the coruler of Pisces is Jupiter, which gives the Pisces male two of the three rulers of the world as his patrons. What this means is that he has more astral divinity behind him than any other sign.

Few people who have met a charming, low-key, Pisces man would suspect he came from as hard a god as Neptune, who is usually pictured as an angry old man. The Pisces male himself appears eternally young. Only his wisdom and rationality give away the maturity and kindness he seems to have had since birth. Poseidon was one of the gods who stood with Zeus and fought against their father, creating the more well-known Greco-Roman pantheon. Again, despite the Pisces man's outer persona of submission, don't doubt for a minute that he's more than capable of bringing down a superior, even if he vacillates a lot beforehand.

One of the most prominent gifts Neptune bestows on the Pisces male is the ability to always change. Neptune was not only the god of the sea, a fluctuating body in itself, but also of horses (whose fluid movements have captivated mankind for thousands of years), and of earthquakes (or, the ability to make that which should be solid and stable flow like the ocean despite its normal state). The Pisces himself is always moving from one situation in life to the next, using the strength of momentum and his ability to move around obstacles as the chief tools to his success. He seems to be the one person in the zodiac who is never caught between a rock and a hard place, and he has difficulty understanding people who just can't seem to escape a negative situation (although he is always willing to lend support). A consequence of his liquidity and lack of black and white thinking is that, like his patron Neptune, he has difficulty making a sexual commitment unless he, unlike Neptune, is able to convince himself that despite all of the rationalizations made by adulterous people, physical relief can have a greater effect than an earthquake on those he loves.

His Top Traits Explored

He's Passive

The Pisces floats through life, enjoying where the universe takes him, but he lacks any overt direction over his own fate. When he wants something, he's incredibly capable of attracting his goals to himself, but he only rarely goes out and seeks. When he does, it's with such detachment that he drives more passionate people insane. His detachment goes far beyond material goals and career ambitions and reaches into his relationships as well. While he loves deeply, he is not passionate. While he is protective, he is not loyal. He understands that there is a variety of interesting people available at all times, so he finds no need to cling to the ones now in his life. He hurts when a relationship fails, sometimes for many years, but his body will move on easily.

Do not mistake "passive" for "submissive." While the Pisces is a drifter in need of some realistic guidance at times, he will never allow someone to move him in a direction he is unwilling to take. The problem is that there aren't many paths he isn't, on some level, willing to take. Although he doesn't mind playing the submissive's role during sex—in fact, he prefers this role as it allows him a lot of freedom to enjoy the encounter—a Pisces man is never truly submissive. At most, he is passive-aggressive and uses deception, emotional ploys, and projection to get what he wants from others. A favorite tactic is forgetting to inform his partner about what he's up to so he can avoid confrontations or directives. This has an extremely negative toll on their relationships because it blocks communication and openness and hinders the ability to work as a partnership.

Sexually, his passivity is the outward result of a vivid inner life. He isn't always aware of the differences between his fantasies and reality, and he has a hard time seeing his partner for who they really are rather than who he thinks or wishes they are or would be. Being socially passive allows him more opportunities to do what he wants and to get away with it.

He's Charming and Disarming

The Pisces male is one of the most trusted, most liked, and most charming in the zodiac. His "wholesome" quality makes it seem impossible that he would ever lie or manipulate someone. He does both readily enough. He believes in courtesy, avoids confrontations or negativity at any cost, and prefers to look at the world through rose-colored glasses. He cannot stand watching others in pain or heartache, and he feels a compulsive need—that he has usually learned to curtail—to help anyone who needs it, which leads to his eventual avoidance of becoming involved with needy people for the sheer fact that he'd become obsessed with helping them.

Unlike the Aries idealist, who always leaves people in a lesser state when compared to his perfect partner, the Pisces idealist sees people and situations in their best light. He gives off the vibe that he honestly likes others with such welcome that the rest of the world can't help but like him back. In the business and social worlds, he doesn't pose an obvious threat to anyone. He's far more ambitious than he lets on, though.

Sexually, he makes women feel loved and cared for. His thoroughness in the bedroom, along with the way he works deep-tissue massage into the sexual equation, exhausts even the most passionate woman, and leaves her feeling like she just had a day at the spa. While he's accommodating enough to thrust hard and heavy a few times, maybe even bruise a wrist or two, he prefers gentle athleticism to BDSM (his previously mentioned enjoyment of being dominated doesn't exactly mean his tail wags for whips or pain).

He's Elusive

The Pisces male is hard to pin down. Commitment, politics, personal beliefs, plans of action, history—you name it. It's not that he's purposely deceitful, it's just that it's so much easier to do what you want if people don't know precisely what they're dealing with, not to mention the fact that it's hard for the Pisces to act or think in black and white terms. As much as he sounds logical and his actions appear to be well thought out, he is an emotional man who is led by his heart (one reason why he tends to partner with authoritative and commanding women).

Besides being emotional, he's also very sensitive to those around him and to the world, and he spends a good deal of energy isolating his bleeding heart from others lest he bleed to death. Because he's soft toward so many causes and so wishy-washy, in general, he usually adopts a belief system that lays down guidelines for behavior. However, he doesn't follow anything beyond "be kind to others" and "forgiveness" sanctions (without which, a Pisces would have found another system to follow). Aside from a belief system, he listens to political standards and the beliefs of his people. He respects and adopts his social doctrine from them—again, finding rules easier to live by than going wherever his emotions lead. Being elusive doesn't make him an ideal companion for someone who is also passive and emotionally driven because no steps would ever be taken towards compromises, bringing up and dealing with hurt feelings, or laying the groundwork for progress. Although he is more than capable of taking the leading role, he finds it uncomfortable sustaining it.

Sexually, his elusiveness is at first a tantalizing challenge, especially when it's coupled with his sensitive hands and mouth and his intuitive understanding of how to make love. Eventually, however, it becomes frustrating that he can't go beyond the sensitive route. Even if he tries, it lacks any real heart, strength, imagination, or longevity.

Sex with a Pisces Male

The Pisces man is a sensitive and caring partner. While he isn't comfortable with rough-and-tumble sex, and doesn't like crudeness, he more than makes up for his lack of machismo by being attentive to his partner's needs and going out of his way to fulfill them. He understands women, and is especially attracted to outgoing, intelligent, and ambitious women because he enjoys bringing out their femininity in the bedroom. He isn't dominant so much as skilled, and he isn't passionate so much as he is detail-oriented and thorough. You can turn to him for a quickie but not a fuck.

It is nearly impossible for him to remove emotion from sex, as he gets most of his sexual response not from the physical enjoyment of the act but from the mental and emotional ones. He spends most of his time in a fantasy world, but not a sexual fantasy world, where romance and true love reign, people are kind to each other, and he is highly successful. While he has more luck than most in turning his fantasies to realities, many of his lovers are unnerved by the reality of the Pisces man. His idea of true love is one that is in no way possessive. Instead, each partner is free to explore their self and the world. He does not think that love requires monogamy, and is willing to agree that a person can be in love with two people at once. While this makes him more understanding of infidelity than many other men would be, it also helps him reconcile his own extramarital activities.

Romance favors big in his sex life. He has an idealistic view of what relationships should be like and being the main care-taker is just the beginning. He doesn't have the drive to become obsessed with his lover like the Scorpio does, and he isn't in love with being in love like a Libra is. He prefers a romance that is sentimental and requires little to no maintenance (although he's very good as a relationship mechanic), one that he can leave and come back to as he feels like it. Being so involved in his own head doesn't make paying attention to life on the outside easy or comfortable, and the Pisces male is all about comfort.

Preferred Games

Mr. Nice Guy

He'll change your tire, walk your dog, talk to you until dawn when you're upset, virtually anything in order to make your life easier. He can make it seem like his one goal in life is being there for others (accompanied with a wry wit and tons of light sarcasm as he's doing it), and he is often taken for granted or used. He'll bend over for you during sex if you want him to, and he isn't aware that he comes off as just a little desperate.

The Jealous Miser

Hard as it may be to imagine, the Pisces has a tendency to be extremely jealous of others who have either the social standing or financial success that he wants to have himself. He can become surly and bullying in his relationships as a result, pushing his loved ones away for fear they think as little of him as he does himself. He can become distrustful and dissatisfied, barking at everyone he meets and generally being as unpleasant as possible.

Don Juan

He loves women, and he loves making love to them. He genuinely appreciates the female body (although he does have certain idealistic preferences about what they look like) and he takes a large interest in finding out how to please each woman he's with. Romance and respect is a part of every move and every touch, and he's a master at subtle seduction. However, like Don Juan, he's also a master at falling in love and leaving. Pleasant memories are enough to sustain him, and he doesn't believe in holding onto love with both fists even if he mourns it for the rest of his life afterwards.

The Uncontainable Man

Even at his job, he can't stand being contained or confined in a space any smaller than thirty acres or so. Give him a corner office with a view, and he'll hardly be in it long enough to appreciate it. In a relationship, he can't stand being held by jealous or restrictive hands. Although he prefers commanding women, he likes them for how they live their own lives and not for how they tell him to live his. If his partner is too confining, he will find a myriad of ways to escape: affairs, a job with traveling, alcohol or drugs, just to name a few.

Absolutely Dreamy

It's hard to tell when this man is awake. Even the most ambitious, responsible Pisces man is performing his duties with only part of his mind and heart. He lives in a world of airy castles in the sky where the world is a utopia. When in a down-to-earth mood, he's so good at sheltering himself from the drabness, unpleasantness, and cruelty that is so often around us that he might as well still be stuck in his head.

What He Needs to Learn About Sex

While he might enjoy slipping out of restrictions, and while he might have difficulty sticking to black and white definitions of what committed men should and should not do, chances are his partner expects certain things from him and by agreeing to commit, he at least needs to find a compromise. His elusiveness can be damaging to both his partner and his partnership. Refusing honest communication is destructive to relationships, as is avoiding confrontations at all cost.

What You Need to Know About
a *Pisces* Woman

February 20–March 20

She moves her hips seductively and yet innocently enough that she could have been doing nothing more than shifting under your weight, then you look into her eyes and see the naked desire there. The reservation is gone, all bets are off, she isn't hiding anything anymore. She wants you and you know it. Your body responds immediately, lips touching hers in a deep, passionate kiss. Her mouth tastes sweet, her tongue invites you to explore and be explored. Oh god! She shifts her hips again, more demanding this time without any of the denial she had before. You groan with desire and cling to her. After a moment, you get to your knees and pick her up before carrying her to the bedroom.

Neptune in Flux

Neptune, or Poseidon as he eventually became, was a god of the sea, and the Pisces woman is forever battling against the waves of her life. Known as the sign of self-undoing for good reason, she has far more trouble with life than her male counterpart, who has learned to relax and go with the flow. Historically, women have rarely been welcomed by the sea, despite or due to the ocean's connection with sexuality (men have been afraid of women's sexuality for quite some time now). And few women have faired well in connection with Poseidon. For example, when Poseidon competed with Athena over the patronage of Athens (by the name alone you should guess who won), Poseidon's gift—a worthless salty spring—did not win against Athena's olive tree, and the city was hers. Another reason the prize was hers is that Athens was a democracy, and the women who voted for Athena outnumbered the men who voted for Poseidon. The rumor is that the men and Poseidon, who sent giant waves at the city, were so upset by the result that they took away the ability to vote from women and so, some say, women's struggle for suffrage began.

The Pisces woman's instability in life results from the instability of her astrological patron, who not only rules the sea, but earthquakes as well. The only place where steadiness may be found, where everything is calm, is at the bottom of the Piscean ocean, deep within herself. Unfortunately, this doesn't promote happiness, as she tends to make poor company for herself. Relationships are next to impossible when one half of the partnership is underwater most of the time. She looks to her partner for what she herself, and her patron, lacks.

Her Top Traits Explored

She Suffers

There is always something weighing on her mind, depressing her mood and keeping her life from what she thinks it should be. She relies on others for relief, as her only method for calming herself is to escape from whatever it is that troubles her. She tends to pick codependent lovers who are so terrified of her retreats, in case it becomes permanent (which isn't such an unreasonable fear), that they are willing to do all of the work to ensure the relationship is successful and she is happy. In short, she has no motivation to take care of herself. While her lover tends to her physical and financial needs, she demands (in her passive Piscean way) absolute freedom to find whatever it is that makes her happy—be it clothes, purses, or other men.

Pisces women are extremely sensitive, and they tend to experience an excessive amount of guilt. This guilt is borne from a vicious cycle in which they do something "wrong," evade any accountability when confronted about it, guilt-trip themselves over the act and the evasion, and then use their guilt as an excuse to commit other "wrong" acts. And, because they aren't comfortable fulfilling society's expectations of them or of love, and they can't think in definitive terms, they have more potential for committing perceived "wrong" acts than more down-to-earth signs. For example, Pisces women often manipulate other because it avoids confrontations. When confronted about their manipulation, however, they'll evade any admission of having done it or they'll blame their partner for giving them no other choice. You should be able to see how the rest of the cycle comes in to play.

Her suffering receives a major spotlight in her sexuality. She has a strong sex drive, and an imagination that makes anything possible in the bedroom. However, her sensitivity to cultural expectations and her own distrust of herself and dislike for the down and dirty realities of life (yes, sex is sweaty; yes, if viewed from a third-person perspective, it can look awkward and humiliating) lead her to restraining her sexual enjoyment and expression with a restraint that is seen nowhere else in her life. She is only comfortable having sex with someone who honestly cares for her and who is gentle and loving. Trust is of huge importance to her, as is security.

She's Nebulous

Not even the Pisces is totally sure of who or what she is. Her persona is generally determined by whomever is closest to her, as well as her own ideas about who she is, for reality begins in her mind. Most of her life is spent in avoiding confrontations and placating others so that she can find the time and support to do what she wants to do. In order to make any real moves in her life, she needs someone there to carry her and make the decisions for her. She's extremely capable of living a successful and happy life as long as someone else is there to take the responsibility for it.

Most of her time is spent in a fantasy world—either the one in her head or the one she's created in her home. Unaware of what reality is, she gleans her information in the same way a person stuck behind a window looking outside would—through the tales, beliefs, opinions, and information of others. Having a serious conversation with her is a headache in itself, for instead of standing behind her opinions and her education (self-taught or formal), she's busy trying to agree with you at every turn, apologizing for whatever tiny disagreement there might be, and then changing her stance entirely if someone new joins the conversation. She does it all without ever noticing her own hypocrisy.

The Pisces female is sexually vague. Her likes and dislikes depend on those of her partner, and if she becomes involved with someone new who is horrified by the bizarre talents on her sexual resumé, she quickly falls back on her pure demeanor and claims it was her ex's fault. She rarely takes the time to figure out what she enjoys, and instead relies on her partner to intuit and provide it.

She's Self-centered

To the Pisces, the world revolves around her and is colored by her emotions. Everything within it is defined by her, because of her, a part of her, and cannot exist without her. She is the eternal toddler, who sees her own excrement as a part of herself and is hesitant to flush. And many of her partners are the exhausted and amused parents, trying hard to keep themselves from pulling the lever just to get it over with.

Every Pisces female believes she is surrounded by lesser people and that they should be grateful to be in her company. She constantly eschews her own perfection and begins a steady psychological war to convince her partner that he is very lucky she spends any time at all with him. She will try, in her soft way, to prove how much more intelligent, honorable, dignified, worldly, and good-looking she is than him, and if he ever proves her wrong she'll pout and whine until he finds himself reassuring her yet again that of course she is far better than he is. The battle of words and emotions with her completely distracts from any actual proof of her superiority that she might have. Claiming supremacy is just the first step in exonerating herself from responsibility.

Sexually, she appears to be self-sacrificing, but the Pisces female never truly gives herself freely to another. There is always a price when it comes to her. The more repressed Pisces sees sex as her duty to her partner and an exchange for the protection her partner affords her. The more outlandish her lover's request, the greater the financial protection she expects. However, when the Pisces' sexuality is carefully cultivated, her freedom in the bedroom and the fun she finds there goes beyond what most other women will ever experience.

Sex with a Pisces Female

The Pisces is a woman you either love or hate. She is seen by some as the last bastion of femininity, the woman every woman should turn to for lessons in how women should behave (i.e., cooking, cleaning, taking care of the children, pampering her husband). Every Pisces woman prefers to have someone else do the actual work, though. She is more like a pampered housekeeper. She is seen as a symbol for everything womanhood once was and should never be again—submissive, passive-aggressive, manipulative, and deceptive. Loving or hating her depends on your own ideals for what women should be—whether you like the modern woman or the traditional one. The Pisces herself finds it hard to reconcile these two opposing views, and she often struggles between outwardly being what everyone wants her to be, and inwardly longing for an unconventional life.

Sexually, the Pisces woman submits to her husband's desires while often repressing her own. Society—the great body she follows to her dying day—does not give her a comfortable release for her sexual energies unless it is through a committed partner who welcomes it. Society's traditional ideal for the married woman is a woman who is always sexually available for her husband, who serves as a receptacle for his need lest he turn to other women. It's a common threat to the woman who does not please her husband regularly in a society that tends to view women as property of their men (a viewpoint that gives security to the Pisces rather than a twist in her womens' rights panties). The Pisces woman tries everything to please her partner. She's willing to wear and do anything to make sure he's satisfied, no matter the mental or physical toll on herself.

Preferred Games

The Weakling

Life is so *difficult*, reality is so *unkind*, work is so *hard*, there's *no point* in any of it. The Pisces woman is famous for defeating herself long before she takes a first step to accomplish anything. It's easy for her to convince others to do everything for her. Once both she and her partner become convinced of her weakness, the only escape is counseling or a breakup. She collects enablers like they're going out of style and usually has one already in position when the other begins to break away.

The Ready-made Victim

She enjoys being dominated in all aspects of life and especially during sex. She gets a secret thrill from being ordered around and even hurt by her partner. It seems to answer some inner masochist/martyr need because she uses it as an affirmation of both her own strength and her partner's "sickness." She has no trouble putting her welfare in someone else's hands and hopes, on some level, that they will fail her.

The Model Woman

Another frequent game of hers is projecting an image of perfection, or at least of blamelessness. If anything goes wrong in her life, she's the last one who deserves the blame because everyone else was against her from the start, and she tried ever so hard to make things right, and it's not her fault if she wasn't good enough. She will always assert that she is the perfect wife, mother, mistress, and friend despite her inner doubts or her actual performance in any of those capacities.

Highly Sexual

Pisces is one of the most sexual signs in the zodiac, and when the Pisces female breaks through her self-repression, there's no telling where, with whom, or how this woman will get her jollies on. It takes a gentle partner, someone who is patient in earning her trust and drawing her out, but when the lid's blown, it's gone. There isn't much she's not willing to try in the bedroom, and when partnered well, the joy she gets from sex is pure heaven.

When It Rains, It Pours

How this woman can cry! Anything and everything has her sitting in her closet or bathroom, blubbering away. She learned at a young age that crying either makes people uncomfortable (so they give her what she wants quickly), or protective (it takes a little longer, but she still gets what she wants and anyone who's hurt her gets pounded), and she uses her tears to her fullest advantage. Anyone who doubts this needs to remember one simple thing: crying—even weeping—requires no noise.

What She Needs to Learn About Sex

She needs to learn to take accountability for herself and her actions. Learning how to define and stand up for what she believes in will help her find stability in her life and attract like-minded people who will benefit her rather than creating her in their own image. Taking an open leadership role in her own life will give her more control and help her feel better about herself while lessening all the guilt that deception gives.